WE'RE NOT LEEDS, WE ARE LEEDS

WE'RE NOT LEEDS, WE ARE LEEDS

DAVE ROWSON

DB
PUBLISHING

First published 2021 by DB Publishing, an imprint of JMD Media Ltd, Nottingham, United Kingdom.

ISBN 9781780916231

Printed in the UK

Contents

Foreword

When that great Leeds United team lost in the European Cup Final of 1975 it marked the end of a period of European football for the club that had lasted for ten years. As the team had grown old together, Leeds then began a slide that would see only a fleeting foray back into European football in 1979. With Leeds's decline resulting in relegation to the Second Division in 1982, more European trips seemed a very long way away.

English teams received a ban from European competitions following the Heysel disaster in 1985. Leeds's pre-season tours and friendlies had often been to Scotland or Ireland, although there were some opportunities to explore further afield with trips to Spain and Sweden of note in 1984. Thankfully, that was all to change again in the 1990s as Howard Wilkinson led the club back to top-flight football and the European ban was also lifted in 1990.

With Leeds now playing some fantastic football under Marcelo Bielsa, it revives memories of the last time we enjoyed entertaining Premier League and European campaigns under the management of David O'Leary with his young team playing fast, attacking football and taking on all comers at home and abroad.

A new generation of fan is now hoping that Bielsa can lead Leeds back into Europe. This book describes, for those who have not had the pleasure of following Leeds in what they have missed and what could await them in the future.

The book is a personal account of following Leeds in Europe, detailing some of the trips that created memories and friendships that have lasted a lifetime. I organised the trips, Rouse Tours as they jokingly became known, which were unofficial and not linked to the club. This allowed for longer stays abroad and a better chance of having a good trip away with nights out and plenty of beers.

The return to Europe starting in the era of Wilkinson – 'Sgt Wilko' – but then also covered five years of European campaigns living the dream with Peter Ridsdale and O'Leary in the late 1990s and early 2000s. A Leeds European tour taking in France, Holland, Belgium, Germany, Italy, Switzerland, Spain, Portugal, Turkey, Russia and Ukraine meant there were games to be played, trips to be arranged and stories to be told upon the return.

'We're not Leeds, we ARE Leeds!' was a statement made at the end of a bar amongst a group of Leeds fans at a game in Europe. Whilst at face value it seems a strange statement, it carried true meaning and feeling when it was made. It signified how it felt at that moment to be a Leeds fan amongst fellow members of the Leeds family in a bar in some far-away destination in Europe.

The book demonstrates how a trip with the lads can result in a wrongful arrest and a stay in a German prison; also how a small thing like this cannot deter a dedicated Leeds fan from following their team around Europe. Side before self, your family and work!

With stories of the many trips recounted in the pub after a few pints, often someone would say, 'You should write a book.' Well, now I finally have. I hope you enjoy reading **We're Not Leeds, We ARE Leeds** as much as we all enjoyed being part of making the stories in it.

Dave Rowson (Rouse)
Member of Harrogate and District Leeds United Supporters' Club

1

Background, Harrogate Branch and Characters

Dave Rowson (Rouse)

A little background about myself, the author. I am a long-time Leeds United supporter, growing up watching the Don Revie team and supporting Leeds home and away since the 1970s. Initially I attended with my father and I was to become a regular traveller on the Pyne's of Harrogate and then Wrays of Harrogate coaches to home and away games.

I had a season ticket with my father from the 1967/68 season in the Lowfields Road seats and travelled with him to away games in the 1970s. With an aunt in the family who worked at the Craiglands Hotel in Ilkley, where Don Revie took the team before home games, we were fortunate enough to manage to get FA Cup Final tickets for Wembley in 1970, 1972 and 1973.

In 1975 for the European Cup Final, I travelled twice to Paris with my father, first via train to buy tickets on sale at the ground and then on Pyne's of Harrogate coaches to attend the game. This clearly must be how I caught the European football travel bug at a very early age.

I branched out on my own at 14 in 1977 when my father stopped going to games and I have continued following Leeds home and away throughout all the ups and downs that have followed.

I am a member of the Harrogate & District branch of the Leeds United Supporters' Club, a former branch secretary, and I was involved in founding it in 1982 (albeit known as Knaresborough at the time).

I have followed Leeds all over, including pre-seasons, testimonial games and friendlies until work, family and my other passion bowling started to

Wrays of Harrogate bus.

intervene and curb the extent of my involvement a little to mainly league and cup games. I was fortunate enough in the main to be able to plan and balance work and leave around attending as many European trips as I could get away with and this book provides my personal account of travelling with Leeds abroad; the people, the situations, the daft things that happen on these trips.

I am still a regular traveller with the branch and I am often seen as a double act with my regular travelling companion, 'Chairman Charley' Megginson, home and away. We are known for liking a beer or two and to enjoy a bit of fun at the games.

This isn't Leeds-related, but we were thrown out of the away section at Wembley in 1992 at the England v Brazil friendly. Not for fighting – we were dancing with the Brazilian ladies and had done the samba into their section with them. We were in there for about ten minutes until we were spotted by the stewards and evicted.

I am now trying to organise a fundraiser in 2021. At the away game against Queens Park Rangers in January 2020, I bought a Stan Bowles Alzheimer's Research UK charity calendar, to be able to get into the home pub on Loftus Road for a pint with Chairman Charley. The calendar also then became a useful birthday present for Sarah White, from the Nottingham Whites, as I had joked that I would get her a cheap one. As she was on the train that day, we were asked to look after 'Stan'. We decided that having your photo taken with 'Stan' would become a thing and random folk were asked, the pictures then appearing on social media. This idea was initially developed just as a bit of fun but it took

Dave Rowson (Rouse).

off on social media amongst fans. I have now decided to use the same theme of a picture with the Stan Bowles calendar with a donation to Alzheimer's Research as a fundraiser once fans are able to return to matches in 2021.

Alzheimer's Research is something close to my heart. Players such as Stan Bowles, Jack Charlton, Jeff Astle, Nobby Stiles and Frank Worthington have had their stories highlighted due to the impact of football as a possible cause. Closer to home, when I ran the supporters' club bus from 1982 to 1987, I lived with my grandmother who developed Alzheimer's so I am aware of the impact it can have on people's lives.

Keeping an eye on the Leeds fixtures, taking phone calls and bookings probably helped slow the onset of the disease a little for my grandmother. However, it did not stop the lads playing a prank. When I returned home from a football kick-about and a few beers my gran had started a list with 20 names on it for an away game against Paraguay. It was during the World Cup and an England match. When I pointed out I thought someone was pulling her leg, she said, 'I thought it was strange you had not mentioned a Leeds friendly game, I thought I had missed it.' Those bookings were quickly referred to Big Mick Hewitt for specialist England and World Cup trips.

Harrogate and District Branch – Leeds United Supporters Club (previously Knaresborough)

Pyne's had operated a pay-as-you-go service to Leeds's home and away games for many years from Harrogate with fans able to turn up at the depot on Camwall Road, Starbeck, or the booking office on Montpellier Hill and just book on for any game. Wrays of Harrogate bought out Pyne's and initially continued to run buses to the away games.

Following damage to the coach at an away game at Old Trafford, Wrays decided to cease this service. Fans had to travel in cars and vans or make their way to Leeds for buses or trains to the games. Following difficulties getting to Wolves for an FA Cup third round tie, the football special being full, I decided that running our own bus was the better option. So for Spurs in the fourth round a Wallace Arnold was hired with a £250 damage deposit. The weeks before involved meeting and collecting £7 off 40-plus folk to cover the costs of the bus. What could possibly go wrong? It was the first trip I ran. To Spurs, into what was the biggest war zone outside a football ground for many a year, and with a £250 damage deposit at stake. It was amazing that the bus escaped unscathed. This trip confirmed my view that we should look to organise regular travel for the following season. Charley Megginson, Mally Appleyard, Will Martin and Kevin Meddings (Jap) were involved at the time in moving this forward.

The Harrogate Leeds United Supporters' Club were approached but the folk running the branch said there was no demand for away travel. We applied to the Leeds United Supporters' Club to set up our own branch but knew that the Knaresborough branch was about to fold. At the executive meeting we were approved to take over running the branch, who had returned £50 to the executive, which was then given to us for branch funds, so we started with £50 behind us. I cannot thank Eric Carlisle enough for the help he gave us setting up and whilst I learnt the ropes running a branch.

I ran the branch from 1982, the first season in the Second Division. Our first game was Grimsby away and the final game was the heart-breaking play-off defeat to Charlton in 1987. We took two buses to many 'local' matches up north, and for the FA Cup semi-final at Hillsborough we took four, then three to Selhurst Park for the Charlton play-off. It was mainly pay on the gate but with no mobile phones and all-ticket fixtures for the semi-final and play-offs it was becoming a full-time job and people were constantly ringing me at work. I think this, coupled with meeting the future wife, meant I decided someone else could have a go and I would just return to being a traveller.

To date, the branch has only had four secretaries organising travel: myself from 1982 to 1987; Pete Gartside 1987–88; Graham Dominy-Ive 1988–2000; and Paul 'Stella' McManus 2000 onwards.

The old Harrogate branch of the supporters' club folded and the

Phil Ashby, Karen Abbott, Dave Rowson.

Knaresborough branch was renamed to the Harrogate and District Leeds United Supporters' Club in 1996 to better reflect our travelling membership.

Ricky Greenwood, Kev Hunt, Andy Yates, Paul Yates, Dave Poole, Andy Logan and Heath Ohiltree.

Harrogate and District LUSC away game.

It would be remiss of me not to mention a few people of note who are still going to the games and/or were travelling friends with Leeds from my past.

From the Pyne's coaches days: the Starbeck branch Karen Abbott, Paul 'Max' Mills, Glen Mills and Andy Logan. Indeed, some of us were on the 1975 European Cup Final trip including 'Chairman Charley' Megginson.

From the front-of-the-bus squad over recent seasons, sharing in the stories that have inspired Lai's blogs, long-time travellers Dave Poole, Mick Hewson, Ken Wood, Steve Smith, and Scarborough exile John Farrell.

Andy Yates, who before the coronavirus pandemic was in the way was on a tremendous run of games, and Ricky Greenwood who along with Little Mick Hewitt seems to be forming the new Covid Whites travel club.

The Harrogate and District branch picks up for away games in Knaresborough, Starbeck, Harrogate and Leeds. Check out www. harrogatewhites.co.uk or search Facebook for Harrogate LUSC Whites for further details.

Sadly, during the period of publishing this book Eric Ware passed away.

I had known Eric from the football since I was four or five years old, he had always been part of my football life.

When I ran the bus, he was our cheerleader. The whole bus would sing 'Eric, Eric, give us a song' and he would oblige with his rendition of 'The Scaffold's song 2 Days Monday'. He was the bus bingo caller – yes we played bingo on a bus of mainly young lads off to football in the 80's. He was famous for his cheerful turns of phrase, commonly raising the excitement of the prize by saying, 'Are you sweating at the back yet?'

My favourite Eric memory was a night match at Everton on Pynes coaches. Only 13 of us were on it I think as it was towards the end of the Adamson Out era. I'm pretty sure Andy Logan and Charley Megginson will have been on board. We were struggling to find the ground, the scousers had nicked their own floodlights and only had them on the stand roof. We ended up on the wrong side of the ground. The bus driver stopped to ask a police inspecto who was standing on his own, directions. He said, 'You go park up, get them off, I will walk them round to the away end'. One copper! Although he did have his big stick thing. Everton was known to be just a little bit rough back then. By the time we had walked about a street, we had all mingled into the Everton fans on the pavements, so that we did not stand out as being Leeds fans. Except Eric, who was still walking behind the copper down the middle of the road with his own personal police escort. If only we had cameras way back then!

Lai Lam wrote recently in tribute:

'At 74 years of age, Eric was the longest standing season-ticket holder in our branch. He would have been 75 in May and we are told had had his season ticket for 40 years. He had been a Leeds United supporter for over 62 years. Eric started watching Leeds in the 1950s and he was one of the few who had the privilege of watching the great John Charles play. Eric was in the crowd of 57,892 people at Elland Road, the biggest attendance at our beloved ground, in 1967 in the cup game against Sunderland.'

Eric has been a member of the LUSC all this time. He was one of the original Harrogate Whites who travelled on the old Pynes buses, back in the day. He travelled home and away all over the country and saw us play in Paris, Salonika and made both Fairs Cup Finals in Hungary and Italy, against Ferencvaros and Juventus.

RIP Eric Ware, a legend of the Harrogate Whites and Leeds United.

A second book may well follow on from this to detail some of the more memorable games and trips domestically and at pre-season games and friendlies with the Harrogate Whites over the years, if I can ever get Chairman Charley to do a Vulcan mind melt direct into Microsoft Word, but this first book will focus purely on the European trips of the 1990s and 2000s and specifically the ones I organised, the Rouse Tours.

First, before the stories of the journeys, an introduction to some of the main characters who feature in the book so that you get a good feel for the quality of traveller that you will encounter along the way.

Stella

Paul 'Stella' McManus, so called due to his early days travelling with the branch when he always got on the bus carrying a pack of Stella Artois. Also still known to some as Mr Artois.

Now the Harrogate branch secretary (of 20 years) and his choice of tipple has progressed, so he may well have been called 'Port' or 'Mr Real Ale' these days. Stella is a great guy and has run the branch for all but five months of this century onwards. He is ably assisted by Lai Lam. The branch still run buses to most away games (tickets permitting). Stella and Lai do a fantastic job of also organising all the other branch activities.

Whilst he is obviously far more sensible now that he is in a responsible position of power and influence, he has had some memorable moments in the past:

Demolishing a chocolate peacock in a hotel foyer at the works Christmas do and waking up in a ditch somewhere in the outskirts of Leeds.

Lai Lam, Paul (Stella) McManus, Peter Hart.

On the way back from a game at Stoke (with his then partner in crime, the Jap) saying, 'We really shouldn't be driving in these dreadful conditions, this snow is awful.' Graham Dominy-Ive, who was driving the van, put the wipers on even though there was not even a hint of snow, thinking he must be missing something. Then when the van stopped for the services mistaking a mini car driving into the services for the Leeds team coach and setting off chasing it across the service station shaking their fists at it (it was a bad defeat). I'm not quite sure which one of them was sick on the bonnet of the only car parked in the car park.

At Arsenal, after a steady drink at Petticoat Lane and on the way back to the bus, running into a market stall and smashing his glasses. When the bus got to Highbury he was stopped by the police near the ground and made up a story that a gang of Arsenal fans had beaten him up, to explain his disorientated state. He gave the gang's descriptions to the police and he was then allowed to continue into the ground.

At Bournemouth in 1990, walking back to our bed and breakfast avoiding gangs of local lads driving around seeking revenge on stray Leeds fans, Charley and I saw a strange sight in a ground-floor window. Stella and Japs room, curtains wide open, lights on, Stella asleep with his feet on the bed and trousers around his ankles (thankfully underpants still on), and his back and head on the floor. Jap was asleep kneeling down with his head on his own bed. Well, it was a promotion night!

On the way back from a game at Crystal Palace he was a little bit tipsy, unless it was travel sickness, and he had thrown up over himself (I should have blamed him in Eindhoven). It had gone all over his jumper. He got off the bus at junction 41 for a night out with Paul 'Smuff' Smith and promptly took the jumper off and threw it in a field. There must have been carrots as a horse in the field then decided to start eating the jumper.

Lai Lam

Rides shotgun with Stella and has been a regular traveller with the branch for many years.

She is a member of the Supporters' Advisory Board, which liaises with the club on behalf of fans, and writes many blogs on the branch site as media and publicity officer.

She never does anything wrong these days and completely denies this story ever happened (sue Charley). After a few drinks on a Christmas Eve in Leeds she shouted off a balcony in a public house, 'Merry Christmas you festive fuckers.' The group of nuns sat below, who were out for a Christmas Eve gathering, looked very shocked.

At a pub stop in Fazakerley on the way to Liverpool for a Christmas match she was undressing 'Porno' Roy whilst sat on his knee as she wanted 'to see his massive scar', so she says. Roy had recently recovered from a major operation and Lai was a health professional. She was clearly interested in his large scar for research purposes. She offered Roy the chance to go into the disabled loo so he could protect his modesty and she could have a proper look. Alas he declined as he was too scared. She only wanted to rub your scar, Roy!

Chairman Charley Megginson

Where do you start with the current chairman of the Harrogate branch? As the psychiatrist in the **Fawlty Towers** episode said, there is enough material for a book right there.

My drinking buddy and sitting next to me on the bus to away games, and there is never a dull moment. Charley has an encyclopaedic memory

Charley Megginson arrives on Facebook.

for dates and events. He can always tell me where we were five, ten, 15, 20, 25, 30 years previously, who we played, where we went, what we had for dinner and what was number one in the charts that week as well.

Currently occupied with his inner circle of ladies – 'They are all after me now that I am for pleasure not for breeding,' he argues – he entertains everyone unless someone or something upsets him, and he needs to have one of his little rants. When I say little, it can last for a whole journey back from London, only being interrupted for his favourite service station and a KFC.

Since joining Facebook in 2018, he has been on a mission to connect with Leeds fans across the world and attractive female singers. His post, 'Today I will be watching Leeds United with the Harrogate Whites', has people hanging on for the stroke of midnight the day before a match from right across the world. Having visited China and appearing on their television he now has eight million Chinese followers.

Charley has so many highlights. Some of them are in the stories in the book but others include:

In 1975 the famous Norman Hunter and Franny Lee fight game he went to Derby on his moped. I remember being on a Pyne's coach aged 12 and hearing everyone laughing as we overtook him. It rained all day long and he was getting sprayed from all the buses and cars.

Turning up at midnight mass in Harrogate drunk every Christmas (I think in the end they had to put bouncers on).

In the Muckles in Harrogate, laying on the floor taking his shoes and socks off and watching the TV. When asked what he was doing he said he thought he was at home in his lounge.

*Charley Megginson – ten-man Wigan day –
Groves, Leeds.*

Running home all the way from Horsforth as he believed there was a ghost in a house where we were crashing down at. The rocking chair in the attic was rocking with no one in it. The lads had told him it was a haunted house with the ghost of an old lady often seen rocking in the chair. Amazing what a little bit of fishing line attached to a rocking chair can do.

He was listening to a World Cup draw whilst performing with one of his inner circle. Just as he reached his moment of climax he heard 'England will play San Marino' on the radio and he let out a loud 'San Marinoooooooooohhh.'

Being followed home from Thomas's nightclub in Harrogate by a lady who took advantage of him whilst he was holding two cups of boiling hot coffee, which he did well not to spill, so he tells us. Then after being the gent and walking her home, two years later worrying that there was a little chairman toddler running around with the lady in question.

More recently, when visiting his now favourite club Fulham in 2019, he won a mystery prize at the turnstile. It involved missing the game, being rushed back out of the ground, and given a ride in a police van plus a free cup of tea and a meal in a London police station followed by a trip on a Megabus overnight to Leeds. Better than Andy Yates's branch raffle prizes, that.

Generally being offended and putting on his blacklist pubs that refuse him admission on the basis that he might just be a little tipsy. How very dare they!

'Porno' Roy

'Porno' Roy Flynn. The membership secretary of the Harrogate Branch but now a very infrequent flyer since the last time we were in the Premier League and had European outings to make. The fastest brush in the north, Roy is the top painter and decorator in Harrogate.

His nickname came about at the Charity Shield in 1992. The branch stayed in a hotel near Regent's Park and the following day, as everyone was on the bus ready to depart for Wembley, the hotel receptionist came and asked if there was a Mr Flynn aboard. 'Yes, here,' says Roy. 'You have not paid for your films, Mr Flynn,' says the receptionist.

Roy claims he fell asleep and others were in his room using the TV and must have accessed the XXX movies. Mud sticks though and the 'Porno' Roy label was born.

Roy's highlights reel includes:

Having survived falling off a roof, major surgery on his back and spine and months in hospital one of his first ventures out was with Stella and I. Returning from a Nottingham weekend on a National Express and about to enter Leeds bus station we all stood up to get off and as the bus turned the corner Roy disappeared. 'Where has he gone?' asked Stella.

'Shit,' I replied. 'Look.' He had fallen down the exit stairs and ended up on his back next to the toilet door with his legs in the air and back against the exit door. Whoops! Not recommended to aid recovery from major back surgery.

Having a day in the Muckles pub for the Cheltenham festival on the beer and, obviously attracted to the barmaid's assets, it all got too much for him and he ended up joining her

Roy Flynn – Membership officer.

behind the bar. I think he thought her bra was about to break as he felt the need to offer her support. Being out of character (according to the landlord), he was warned as to his future behaviour and got away with a reprimand. Roy sent her a lovely big Easter egg with a bow and everything as an apology.

However, it was his birthday shortly after and he had arranged a break to Budapest. We wound him up whilst on the trip that we had sent a postcard to the pub addressed to the barmaid concerned, saying he was enjoying thinking of her drizzling the chocolate from his Easter egg over her assets.

We stayed in Budapest on a moored ship that we christened the 'love tug'. Roy was single and despite the staff asking us to go to a party onboard that night he wanted to go to a music bar with some others in the travelling party. The rest of us went to the party on the boat – it was literally a boat full of women! Unlucky, Roy. It was a singles night and 90 per cent of the attendees were ladies, which is why the staff were so keen for us (well, a group of blokes) to come to the party. If Roy fell into a barrel of women's breasts, he would still come out sucking his thumb, and his second nickname was born, 'Pleasure Dodger'.

His party piece is to pass out. He did it on the bus coming back from a game and it was like a scene from the film **Airplane**. There was a queue of people waiting in line to punch and hit his chest trying to revive him. On another occasion he did it in the Muckles pub in Harrogate. When he came around, he was lying on the floor with his head in the lap of the resident Scottish doctor, Dr Death, who was stroking his head. Bizarrely the doctor, Doug, who drank in there with his other half, was actually Roy's real doctor. As Roy raised an eyebrow and looked up at Doug stroking his head, he looked quite bemused. Roy did not want to wake up with his head on your lap Doug, he was hoping it would be your wife stroking his head, we joked.

He clearly likes receiving treatment (other than from Lai) as he once had an attack of cramp on a bowling green and before you could blink, an elderly guy had his shoe and sock off stroking his foot whilst he lay in the middle of the green. Porno Roy would normally pay good money for that!

Toby and Boycey

Toby and Boycey were a double act often described as 'the brutal brothers' due to their reputation for crazy days out on the beer.

They were inseparable and on one occasion when they had been apart for a week or so they greeted each other so enthusiastically, in the local pub, that they were like two dogs meeting. They were circling each other rubbing noses and nuzzling each other; we really thought they were going to lick each other's faces.

They were true partners in crime and once met are never forgotten. Boycey got Toby in a few scrapes. He was always causing an altercation and then it was Toby who copped for it.

In Heerenveen pre-match they were sat at a table for a meal with two other Leeds fans. One of the lads says to Toby, 'Can you stop your mate staring at me, he's putting me off my food.' In the ground Boycey managed to upset some other lads in the toilets and Toby had to get involved. He says, 'Next thing I know I'm on the floor lying in the trough with a police dog in my face.'

On a night out in Leeds they both ended up in an ambulance from the Viaduct pub. Boycey decided to insult someone's wife and next thing the bloke had him 'holding him up and hitting him like a hammer hitting a nail', says Toby, who again wades in to the thick of the fray to try and save his mate. Toby then gets an ashtray around his head for his troubles and they are both

Stephen (Toby) Boyes, Andrew (Boycey) Boyes.

carried out and taken to A&E in an ambulance. I was just up the road in the Hogs Head and went looking for them. It sounds like it was good timing that I missed them. They did get an apology and a pint out of the incident at a future Leeds game as the lads who did it were told they were 'good lads'.

On a stag do in Barcelona I turned up a couple of days after the others and found them in an African bar. They have been buying stuff off a guy in the bar, 'think it is Persil' says one of the lads, and I could see why as they were wandering around pissed up frothing at the mouth with bubbles coming out.

In Prague on my 40th birthday trip, they had demanded that they wanted accommodation less than £10 a night, I delivered but it was a little out of town. Checking in, we all met up in a bar next door to the hotel. Boycey came storming in, 'Rouse there was no bog roll in the room!' 'Well you wanted cheap, there's a woman at a desk you can get them there.' 'It's not on no bog roll in the room, you know what Toby's arse is like!!'

Boycey

Boycey is often described as the Dr Jekyll and Mr Hyde of the touring party.

'I am a nice person,' he often says. 'Whoever told you that is lying' was a regular response from one of the travelling group. He can be when sober but other times he could be a complete nightmare and need looking after and keeping on a very short leash.

We were always amazed he did not get smacked more often as he was always in people's faces and asking them questions in an intrusive and what could have been perceived if you did not know him as an aggressive manner. He looked quite a scary character though on first sight and it was mainly out in Leeds, from Leeds fans, that he got a smack.

Plenty of Boycey highlights are in the book, but a few others include:

After the branch won the Leeds United Supporters' Club seven-a-side competition, goalkeeper Pete Gartside was injured. Boycey was talent-

Boycey.

spotted during the early-morning kick-about on Yarmouth beach. 'You look like you can play in goal?' 'Yes, I played for Compton Arms in Leeds.' 'Right, you are in the national finals next weekend.' He was brilliant and we beat Liverpool in the final to win it. Boycey made a brilliant save in the top corner to keep it 2-0.

On a trip to Scarborough staying at a B&B and when Boycey was drunk, Dougie Kaye thought they had him safely in bed in the bunk trapped by the ladder. Then the landlady appeared, waking Dougie up, and said, 'Can you come and get your friend please, he is in our quarters in the bath.' Dougie went upstairs with her and she led him to the bathroom. Boycey was laid in the bath, asleep on his back with his knob in his hand. Dougie got him up and tried to help him back to their room. Boycey was drunk and he was struggling to walk. As they made their way downstairs their legs got entwined and they fell down the stairs full-length, ripping off the handrail and a shelf on the wall at the bottom. Next morning, when he woke up, Boycey said, 'Are we off for breakfast?' The rest just wanted to get out as fast as they could.

On a stag do in Barcelona he had a bad case of mistaken identity and had a pooh in the bidet. He then left the tap running and flooded the room. Toby had got out of bed slipped and he said, 'There were big turds floating around by my head. It was like a horse had been in there!' The next night he made the same mistake again. Toby says, 'The cleaner was just waiting with the mop! She knew what was coming.'

Boycey, Dougie, Rouse, Guy Bernard, John Reaveley and Chris Allison – in Prague.

On a trip to Prague for a lads' weekend, towards the end of the first night there was a wide road that had cars and tram tracks to avoid. Toby, Boycey and I ran to get across and it seemed we all were across the road and on the pavement. Then, whack – Boycey was hit by a tram. A tram had sounded its bell as a warning as we ran across the road and Boycey, turning to give it the V, was hit by another tram nearest the pavement coming in the other direction.

As his head hit the floor there seemed to be a delay and then a pool of blood about a yard wide slowly appeared from his ear. He was just lay there and Toby said, 'He's fucked!' which I took to mean he might be nearly dead. I said, 'It would appear that way.' We were convinced he was dead. Then after about a minute he did a sit up that the wrestler Undertaker would have been proud of. He shook his head from side to side and made a noise like a roar. The ambulance took him to hospital. After a couple of days, he discharged himself as he did not want to be left behind and got on the plane home with the rest of us. He looked like he had been three rounds with Mike Tyson and was clearly still very concussed. At the airport he was talking about a comedian, I think it was Frankie Howerd, and said, 'I'm free!' then burst out laughing. So his head was clearly still scrambled as he had his catchphrases all jumbled up.

Dougie, Roy and Rouse checking on the tram.

On a Benidorm trip he could not find his room. He was sharing with Toby but ended up trying to get in everyone else's rooms. In the end one of the lads went with security to reception with him and they were showing him the passports they had to find his room-mate and room number. When they showed him Toby's passport he said, 'I've never seen that bastard before in my life!'

Toby

Bramley-born and now an immigrant of Harrogate. He is well known on the local football and cricket circuit. I met Toby playing Sunday football.

He had always been a Leeds fan and has many a story about rough old away games in the 70s.

Renowned for contradicting himself in the same sentence and saying a few bizarre things, some of his highlights include:

Whilst Toby was running the line as player-manager, a young lad picked up the ball on the wing. Toby shouts, 'Get on your horse!' The confusion on the lad's face was priceless, he couldn't run for thinking, 'What the hell did he say?'

Toby.

At the first training session of a new season everyone met on the Stray in Harrogate near the Muckles pub. About five new lads had come along. We were about to start to play a practice match, but someone said, 'We can't play here, look at all this dog pooh everywhere on the pitch.' 'What's up, it's dry,' says Toby, picking it up and throwing it off the pitch. He then proceeds to walk up to the five new lads offering his hand to shake saying, 'Hi, I am Toby'.

We played at Ripon on a caravan site and had to get changed at the side of the pitch as we were late. Toby had his boots, socks and shin pads on but nothing else and was stood having a piss in a bush. A car came driving down the road from the caravan site. 'Toby, there's a woman in this car,' someone shouts. He turns around with his dick in his hand just as the car drives past with the woman looking out the passenger window and the kids in the back.

He was sent off in a game with an opponent for fighting and they climbed over the barbed-wire fence and slugged it out in the cabbage patch. The ref had to stop the game whilst we all watched.

Hearing that a bloke at my work was nicknamed 'Sausage', he asked why. I said he was into amateur dramatics. One of blokes given him the name, which I think is short for Sausage Jockey. Toby says, 'I would be proud to be called a sausage jockey! ''Really, what do you think it means?' I asked. 'That you shag around!' he answers. I never did get him the t-shirt with 'proud to be a sausage jockey' on it.

His ex-wife phoned him late at night from abroad and he was sat on the stairs at home in his dressing gown. He reckons she was talking dirty to him and he had not realised that wine was spilling on him in an intimate area until the dog decided to start licking it off him.

One Christmas we were away at Liverpool and had two buses stopping at a working men's club in Fazakerley. It was a lunchtime kick-off and we were there very early. Looking at the crowd of people at the bar, Toby says, 'This landlord must think it's Christmas!!' Looking up at the decorations everywhere someone says, 'It is Christmas, you daft bastard!'

Dougie Kaye

El Presidente, named at the time he was president of the Harrogate Conservative Club.

Dougie was another following Leeds from the 70s and has some of his pictures from the Amsterdam pre-season tournament in one of Heidi Haigh's books. He has some stories from the really old days and keeps threatening to put these in a book of his own.

Well known for his love of Sam Smith's pubs, and with his belief that you can 'smell the mark-up' in fancy places he will always attempt to take you on a five-mile walk to save ten pence on a pint.

He is famous for a picture in the national papers from Derby away when

he was dressed in the **Clockwork Orange** gear.

Having a residence in Portugal, he decided to go over with Toby, Boycey and Mick Povey during the European Championship finals in 2004. Hearing reports of England fans being stopped at the airport, Dougie decided he would dress so they would not associate him with the football. 'Bloody hell! It's David Niven,' they

El Presidente in Harrogate Cons.

said as he turned up in cream chinos, a blazer, cravat and a straw boater hat. 'We need to keep a low profile,' says the English gentleman.

I'm not sure it was ever going to work with the other three in tow. At Leeds Bradford Airport, as the police stopped a group of lads and questioned them, Toby stood waiting behind them. 'What are you doing?' asked the copper. 'We have not asked to speak to you.'

Five minutes after they started serving drinks on the plane, Mick, who is sat next to Dougie, decides to spill a glass of red wine all over the cream chinos.

When they get out of the customs checks in Portugal, they come out the front of the airport and find Toby having a leak against the wheel of an ambulance.

On another trip to Dougie's villa, they met a group of Millwall fans in a bar who were on a golf trip. There were about 20 from Millwall and just the four from Leeds: Dougie, Toby, Boycey and Porno Roy.

The Millwall lads are drinking shots through their eyes and being generally raucous. They tell our boys that Leeds had attacked 'women and children' when they got run back into the South Stand at a game at Elland Road. 'You did not have any with you,' say our lot.

Dougie and Boycey.

There are three big Portuguese skinhead bouncers in the bar that the Millwall lads have been talking to and have sent over to suss out the Leeds fans. They, however, take a liking to our boys, buy them a beer and say, 'If it kicks off we are with you guys.'

Later in the night some women want them to get in a car to go to a nightclub. Dougie says they are not getting in any car. Of course, Toby and Boycey do and disappear into the night. The bouncers in the club think Toby and Boycey are mental as Boycey spends most of the time heading the wall. Meanwhile, Dougie and Porno Roy share a hot chocolate on the apartment balcony while awaiting their return.

At one of the FA Cup games against Arsenal, Dougie heads up to the ground without a ticket. He comes across a Leeds fan being wrestled to the floor by the police. Just before he is carted away, Dougie manages to get his match ticket out of his hand and says, 'That will not be any good to you where you are going.'

Now you have a feel for some of the characters involved in these trips so let us get on with the tales of the actual journeys themselves.

2

Stuttgart and Barcelona, 1992

Following our promotion in 1990 and the title win in 1992 the good times were back. A visit to Wembley for the Charity Shield seemed like the icing on the cake but we had also qualified for the European Cup, and had this to look forward to.

Leeds had been drawn against German champions Stuttgart. The official trips did not look that appealing as they were only offering a limited time in Germany, which did not appear to leave much time for refreshments and would probably result in us being herded straight into the ground. We decided to go give Unofficial Football Tours (UFT) a go as they were advertising trips, even though they were Mancs of the Red variety, run by two brothers John and Geoff. There is a whole book about these guys – **Scum Airways** – which we'll be hearing more about later.

We booked on, and the itinerary was to fly to and stay in Frankfurt and then from there to be transported by bus to Stuttgart for the game and then return by bus back to Frankfurt (or so we thought).

I travelled with Mally Appleyard (at that time my future brother-in-law), Kevin Meddings (the Jap, where is he now) and Paul McManus (Stella) of Harrogate Whites. After booking in to the hotel, we went for a couple of beers in the local bars and then boarded the bus at the agreed time and headed for Stuttgart. The bus headed into the centre of Stuttgart to drop us off for a few beers, with the ground being quite a way out of the centre.

There were a lot of Leeds fans around so we had an enjoyable time and quite a few beers on our pub crawl. Language was an issue for us and

Kevin (Jap) Meddings, Charley and Nigel Fawcett.

the Jap, who thought he had German mastered, ordered a burger with all the trimmings. What arrived was raw fish of some description, much to our amusement. Raw fish in Germany would come back to haunt me later in my Leeds-supporting career.

We went back to board the bus and our 45 or so had turned into a party of about 60 for the trip to the ground. Leeds fans saw this as a better option for getting to the ground quickly than making their own way. We set off and the travelling party was very loud and lively; in fact many were as pissed as farts. The driver was agitated and not very happy with the boisterous travelling group. The party got louder and more vocal as we got closer to the ground and I thought the windows would go through, with one passenger continually braying the window and continually shouting, 'We're Leeds aren't we!'

We started to get quite near the ground and a few Stuttgart fans could be seen on the paths. As we drove down one road two teens, probably 16 or 17 years old, were flashing the V and doing hand signals at us. One of the more drunk passengers screamed for the driver to stop the bus, which he would not do even when he was asked twice, and I could not believe what happened next. The passenger punched the driver and the bus lurched into the edge of the pavement and came to a stop. The bus's front and middle doors opened and a comedy moment occurred. One passenger leapt off the front and one off via the middle door. As they saw

Jap, Val Rowson, Paul (Max) Mills and Mally Appleyard.

each other they ran and attacked each other; it was comedy gold. The German kids had long gone and the Leeds fans off our bus were so pissed that they had clearly thought each other was a German who was already on the street.

The driver refused to travel any further and go to the ground (I do not know why) so we all disembarked, and the bulk of the party, who were clearly very drunk and up for a party, set off for the stadium. We decided to hang back a little and make our way a little behind to avoid getting instantly locked up.

We could tell the group had found a party with the locals by the sound of the helicopter hovering in the air above and the sound of sirens and police dogs as we got nearer to the ground.

When we were there, it was a like we were in a 1970s time warp. All the locals were fully decked in red and white hats and had scarves hanging from their wrists and they were all dressed in denim jeans and jackets. There were thousands of them hanging around. We stuck out a mile in our plain clothes and small Leeds lapel badges. It got quite lively with sporadic fights breaking out as the German fans started attacking the smaller groups of Leeds supporters who were making their way to the ground and in the melee our little group got split up.

As we reached the corner of the ground, I was with Mally. As we got to the area directly outside the stadium there was a huge group of Stuttgart fans hanging around, hundreds of them, but also a phone box and Mally suddenly declared, 'I promised to phone Rebecca today; I haven't yet,' and disappeared into the phone box, leaving me stood outside waiting for him like a spare part. If, when he came back out, he was going to emerge as Superman to take on all comers, I could have lived with that. He was in there for five minutes and I had already had a few Stuttgart fans looking me up and down suspiciously and the fights were still breaking out in the throng every few minutes. There was no sign of him coming out. I decided it was every man for himself, that Mally had his ticket, so I'd leave him to it. He was at least in a shark cage whilst I was treading water waiting for the attack from behind.

I made my way around the ground to find the Leeds section, and bumped into a few familiar faces on the way. It was lively inside, too. There was a pen of Leeds official tickets in one corner of the end, a pen of pay-on-the-day fans in the other corner and a middle section that seemed to be mixed with both sets of supporters. You also seemed to be able to swop between the middle and far pen (a bit like trips to Highbury used to be on the Clock End), and it seemed designed to assist with the fighting.

Leeds played very poorly on the night. Eric Cantona gave the ball away far too often and cost us a goal before limping off later in the game. We went down 3-0 and our European tour looked like being a very short one. There was also sporadic fighting in that middle section during the match.

As the game ended, we realised that we had no clue where or if the bus would pick us up. We found some of our touring party and our Manc tour guides and proceeded to circle the ground looking for the bus. We found more of our party and ended up with a good 30-plus of us wandering the streets. There were groups of Germans hanging around. 'Come on Leeds if they want some, we'll give them some!' piped up Geoff the Red tour leader. Our party must have had a deterrent factor as the locals gave us a wide berth. We found the Leeds coach park and most of the rest of our party but there was no sign of our coach. We were directed to another coach park but no luck. As we stood in a street at the far side of the stadium, out of nowhere two large police vans arrived. About 20 riot cops formed a semi-circle and walked towards us with the intention of holding us where we were in the street.

John the second Red appointed himself as chief negotiator and started speaking to a character who looked a bit like Inspector Clouseau the way he was dressed. Clouseau appeared to be in charge. A few calls were made by him based on whatever story he was being told about the fans being abandoned by the bus company for no reason. Clouseau asked John the Red about any trouble on the way to the match. Perhaps the bus company may have mentioned something they were not happy with. He turned to look at the group of 30 or so assembled behind him, and said, 'Do these lads look like the sort of lads who would cause trouble?' I nearly started laughing out loud, I was thinking that would be a big fat YES.

After about 20 minutes and a lot of phone calls it appeared clear that the bus driver had decided that he would not be returning and that he would not drive us back to Frankfurt. There was also no prospect of getting another bus from the company. Clouseau said, 'I am not sure what you have done but they seem to be upset with you.'

As we were thinking about what would happen next, the police all seemed a little perplexed, then about six more vans of riot cops arrived. They got out of their vans, drew their batons and walked towards us in a large semi-circle so no one could get out of the way and the circle was getting smaller the nearer they got. 'Right lads, they are going to give us it, get ready!' said one of our party.

It turned out that a potential police beating was just a false alarm. In fact it was exactly the opposite as Clouseau had clearly fallen for the Red's gift of the gab, and the police had decided to give us an escort to the train station. They took us via a local train from the ground into the main Stuttgart station and put us on a train back to Frankfurt. Clouseau had issued us with a handwritten note telling the train guards we should get free travel back to Frankfurt as our transport had let us down and we had no money to pay!

As we got on the train, I was reunited with Jap, Stella and Mally, who had made the same trip to town under their own steam but had managed a few beers while dodging the fighting going on in the city centre. Despite me being very jealous of the beers they had managed to obtain they had had to pay for their train tickets back to Frankfurt, so I guess everything evened itself out.

The next day we had a few beers in Frankfurt before heading home and were expecting a quiet time. However, we were wrong, and we went into a little back street bar where it was not to be quiet despite being almost devoid of customers. We were sat chatting about the events of the day before, on and off the pitch, when we saw some strange wizardry. A couple of the local men had got some darts from behind the bar and started throwing them at an electronic machine in the corner. We had just seen our first electronic dartboard. Those Germans are clever at technology. We proceeded to have a debate about how the bulbs were not getting damaged and how people were not electrocuted retrieving the darts.

Either our stupidity or ignorance must have offended one of the locals. The Germans must be the loudest folk in the world and a guy in workmen's clothes at the bar and the barmaid had the biggest row ever, shouting and screaming at each other. From the 'Auslander' word he kept shouting I reckon he did not want us occupying this corner of Germany. We were spending many marks on our beers and the barmaid firmly put him in his place so he left the bar and not us!

We returned to England without too much further disturbance. It had been quite an experience and despite a poor result a memorable trip for our return to Europe.

* * *

The home leg was one of the most memorable games at Elland Road, and we won 4-1, although it should have been 5-1 as we had a Chapman header that hit underside of the bar and looped behind the line before coming out of the net disallowed. So we were out on away goals having thrown the kitchen sink at them.

Next thing we know there is news that Stuttgart have fielded an ineligible player on the night as by bringing on a foreign player off the bench they exceeded the allowed quota, and the verdict of UEFA is that we are ordered to play a one-off game to decide who goes through. It was to be played in Barcelona, and I think we were given four days' advance notice. My Mrs, Val, said, 'The only way you are spending that much again so soon on a European trip is if I go too.' So it was Barcelona here we come.

Once again, the Mancs sorted it out. I had to meet the Unofficial Football Tours guy at Elland Road midweek to pay and then arrange to pick up the flight tickets from him in Stockport. We travelled to Stockport, stopping with one of Val's friends overnight, then drove to Birmingham for the flight to Barcelona. There was one other Leeds fan, Steve, a fireman from Birmingham, on our trip. He now lives in Guiseley. The UFT guy met us at the airport in Spain and took us via taxi to the hotel in the heart of Barcelona.

After a few bars we made our way to the ground. It was strange being in the Nou Camp that night – a 100,000-capacity stadium with around 3,000 Leeds fans at one end, around 2,000 Stuttgart at the other end, and a smattering of neutrals. Whilst it was an impressive bowl to watch the game from, under the stands the stairs reminded me of Roker Park, and the ground looked like it was about to fall down. The facilities toilets and food outlets could not cope with a crowd of 3,000 in our end; maybe they were not expecting that many!

During the match we sat near the UFT guy and I am pretty sure he was on something. He did a crazy celebration when Strachan scored. He went full-on Phil Hay, doing a Brazillianesque 'Gooooooooooaaaaaallll' shout as he gyrated in a very strange manner. In a memorable night on the pitch Carl Shutt scored the winner and we were through to the next round.

We adjourned to the bars of Barcelona and decided to have a pub crawl back into town. Whilst we were sat outside a bar under a canopy the heavens opened; what a storm there was that night! It was just like a monsoon. We were stuck in the bar not far from the ground for a few hours until it stopped.

We relocated into the centre of town during a rain break and then off it went again, so we were stranded in another bar for a few hours more and bumped into Steve, our fellow traveller. We were only yards from our hotel but as he decided to go back there we did wonder if he would make it. He must have been 6ft 4in at least and was doing a cross between an impression of Bambi on ice and a pissed giraffe. He held on to every door frame, sign and lamp post between the bar and the hotel as we watched

Dave & Val Rowson.

to make sure he made it back safely. Just as well we did, based on what we found out the next day.

We had breakfast and then headed to drink in the square just off La Rambla. Leeds fans were sharing their experiences of the Moroccans on the streets the night before, who were trying to pickpocket or mug people all over the place. Even as we sat listening to the stories one of them tried to take a bag from the floor next to the table. When he was stopped from taking it, he did a circle of the square, came straight back and tried again. It was only a threat to knock him out that prevented a third attempt.

Later in the afternoon, Val and myself decided to have a walk along the sea front but had not realised how far we had gone. On the way back we thought there must be a short cut and decided to cut through and go as the crow flies back to the area where we were staying. This was a big mistake and we found ourselves in a rat run of high buildings with narrow streets. It became increasingly clear from the people on the streets and the few small shops and cafés that we were in the home territory of the Moroccans.

It is bizarre, the difference you feel on your own or with the Mrs. I would not have given much of a concern for my own safety if on my own. Mrs R was getting a bit more nervous as there were more and more Moroccan men on street corners and outside little cafés and bars. I had tried to pretend I was not bothered, and it was nothing to worry about but as we approached a corner with a bar there were about 12 of them were covering the width of the narrow street so my cover dropped and I said, 'We are not far from the square now, you go through first if owt happens, just leg it. I'll slow them down.' Despite seeming very reluctant to move out of the way at first, I think because we had no bags, no phones (those were the days), no cameras, watches or jewellery visible they eventually parted.

Stella was not quite so lucky that night. He was in the process of getting mugged by a group of Moroccans just off the main street when Collar flew to his rescue and got rid of them.

Do not be put off as Barcelona is a lovely city and the locals are mainly friendly if you stay on the main drags.

The next game was against Rangers – the Battle of Britain. There was a ban on away fans and that would normally have made me more determined to go, but I had a work commitment that I could not get out of so I did not make the trip. Although I then suffered John Lukic's horror punch and the Strachan disallowed goal along with everyone else on the TV.

As the second leg approached, I ran into a bit of an issue. I had been a season ticket holder every year but due to the European trips, paying for the East Stand bond £500 and having a new house to pay for, I decided I could not afford the money up front to buy a season ticket that year. I would pay on a match-by-match basis. I went down to the ground to get a ticket to be told I was not eligible for one and would have to just wait in the free for all, only season ticket bond holders and fully paid-up bond holders would get priority, and not individual bond holders paying monthly. To say I was not happy was an understatement. Monica, the manager, suggested I bought a season ticket there and then or pay off the balance of my bond which was on direct debit over five months, and it would be problem solved.

I pointed out to her I had just spent about £1,000 following Leeds to Stuttgart and Barcelona plus I was paying £500 for a bond. 'I am a bond holder,' I argued.

Monica's reply was staggering, 'When you have a mortgage for a house it's not yours until you've paid it off.'

'No that is true, but you can bloody live in it!' was my angry reply.

To get my ticket, I wrote to club chairman Leslie Silver and suggested he put Monica on a customer care course. My ticket duly arrived in the post with an apology from him which was fair enough.

We managed to lose the Battle of Britain. Leeds were unlucky in Scotland and while Rangers played well at Elland Road, Mark Hateley had the performance of a lifetime and would have scored that goal once in a thousand attempts if that.

Still, it was a good campaign in Europe in 1992 with a bonus replay thrown in and some thoroughly enjoyable trips.

3

Monaco, 1995

We were back in Europe after a two-season break and I was really looking forward to our trip to Monaco in the UEFA Cup. The Harrogate (Knaresborough at that point) branch were taking a bus to this one. In the build up to the game we had a Friday wedding to attend followed by a game away at Spurs on the Saturday.

On the Thursday night before the trip, disaster struck. Six of us had not received our away cards back and the branch had been told to expect strict security checks at all ferry ports following lots of trouble abroad involving England and various clubs at that time. We suggested we could jump off the bus and board as foot passengers before getting back on the bus at the other side in France having left the ferry. This was rejected by Graham Dominy-Ive, who was running the branch at the time, as being too risky. So the six of us were told we could not travel with the branch.

For five of them, that was that, they were not going. However a travel ban has never stopped me too often in the past (Carlisle and Wimbledon spring to mind) and I decided alternative arrangements would be made even if it meant me going on my own. I found a return train ticket from Leeds to Nice at £144 which was not a bad deal. This included a SeaCat crossing and a sleeper train with bed for the overnight return legs between Paris and Nice.

Having sorted all my arrangements and then done the day-long wedding do on the Friday, I set off for Spurs on the train. After arriving in London and jumping on the tube, I walked from Seven Sisters thinking, 'This walk is not quite what it used to be!' When I got to the ground, I had a problem with the stewards. I did not have an away card so they decided they would not let me in. 'It is in the post' was not a good enough answer.

I was hanging around outside thinking up my next strategy to get in, like to try again shortly. A minibus full of lads turned up at the away end. They said their cards had not turned up in the post and were arguing with the same steward. 'Hey, there's Graham from the Leeds supporters' club branch, he will vouch for us,' they said, pointing and shouting at me. I was beckoned across and asked to sign on a clipboard to vouch for them. I duly signed as Graham Dominy-Ive and got them and me into the ground. I was shaking my head in disbelief as this was the same steward who had turned me away moments earlier. I was obviously not that memorable and he was no Phil 'Thumbs Up' Cresswell, clearly! So, whilst Graham had bumped me from the bus, I guess he did get me into the ground. I cannot remember much about the game other than it was a 2-1 defeat and Tony Yeboah scored. I had a few beers in the pubs to Seven Sisters on the way back into London and I stayed over Saturday night ready to board the train at Charing Cross.

Sunday I was up early and off for the train to Felixstowe, a SeaCat across the channel to Calais, then a train to Paris and on to Nice. In Charing Cross there seemed to be a few small groups of lads dotted around but no one I recognised. When we got on the SeaCat, surprisingly, I headed for the bar and this was where I met three Leeds fans from Bristol and a lad travelling on his own from Horsforth called Blockhead. We downed a few pints and had a good natter. We then got the train from Calais to Paris and arrived about 4pm, so we had about five hours until the sleeper train to Nice which left from another station in Paris. We decided to drink near to that station to make life easier as there would be less chance of missing the train.

Getting to the station, we took one look at the café bars and thought no way, as Dougie Kaye would say, 'You can smell the mark-up!' so we headed into the back streets. We were in an Arabic area and found a tiny little bar with barely room for two people to pass inside. It had an impressive ladder down into to a cellar where no doubt folk had hidden from the Germans in the war. The five of us stayed and drank for a few hours, so the staff had to make frequent visits to the cellar to restock our supply of bottles. There was a famous footballer drinking in there too – Graeme Souness! Well, an Arab with a moustache and a bushy perm who looked a dead ringer.

When it was time to go for the sleeper train the staff made another trip for a crate of beer. They insisted that we took the crate free of charge for the trade we had given them. They said, 'This is for you for the train!'

Our newly formed band of travellers got to the station and somehow managed to get on the train. We had allocated rooms that contained four bunk beds in, so we shared the beers out. The Bristol lads headed one way and Blockhead and I were at the other end of the train. Blockhead decided he did not want to be on his own so came to drink his beer in my room. He stood up (well, was propped up by a ladder to the top bunk) in my room. The Chinese fella reading his book on his bunk was not too impressed with Blockhead periodically letting rip with several massive farts. His arse was very close to where the bloke's head was as he read his book on the bottom bunk.

Blockhead, all blown out after a long day, eventually retired to his own room. When I woke up early, I went on to the corridor and there was a beautiful view of the coastline of France along the Mediterranean. It was quite stunning.

Leeds had advised against fans travelling, saying tickets for the game would be £50 and the cheapest drinks £5 and the accommodation would be hundreds of pounds. At that time, we were never ones to believe the club statements about away European travel. It was as if they did not want us to go.

We arrived in Nice at 9am and there were a lot more Leeds fans on board than we realised as it seemed the people getting off were all groups of lads carrying their travel bags. We headed to find some accommodation and we were directed to one just down the main road from the station. A few York lads, having heard the horror stories peddled by the club, had emptied their banks. Asking the cost of a room at reception they kept saying, 'Is that all? Can we upgrade please? We were told it was expensive!' They kept upgrading until in the end they took the penthouse suite as it was nearer to what they had budgeted for. A basic twin room was about £12 each per night, not £50 per person said by Leeds. Where did that come from?

We checked in to the hotel, where I was sharing with my newly found friend Blockhead. As were unpacking he suddenly, Crocodile Dundee-style, pulls out a huge sheath knife from down his hiking socks. Yes, he was dressed in hiking boots, woolly socks, big shorts, a sort of string vest and a bandana. He was a big lad and certainly a larger-than-life character.

Our next conversation went along the lines of:

'What the hell are you doing with that? Did you come through customs with that on you?'

'Yes, I bring it with me for protection when I am travelling alone!'

'You are liable to get stabbed with it yourself if they take it off you. Leave the bloody thing in the room, you are not on your own now!'

We had agreed to head to Monaco and see if we could get our hands on the £50 match tickets. We proceeded to meet up in reception with the Bristol lads and headed to the station for the short journey on the train.

We had a quick trip to the marina and were taking in the sights of the array of yachts and the beautiful people who seemed to be heading on and off them. We were admiring a large boat that had three speed boats attached to each side of it. There was a guy polishing the boat who spotted us and came over for a chat. He was an Aussie. It was not his boat, but he reckoned the cost of it was in the millions, not the hundreds of thousands. There was a pub next to the marina so we decided we would pop in for a pint. It was £4.50 a beer and the most expensive pint we bought on the trip but still not as much as the £5-£10 rumours put about by the club. We stayed for a couple of drinks as the beautiful people wandered in and past while we sat looking out to sea, sitting on the dock of the bay. Blockhead fitted right in with these surroundings in his hiking boots, woolly hiking socks, massive shorts, string vest and bandana.

We headed up to the ground and managed to lay our hands on some match tickets for £10 a pop openly on sale for the Leeds end. Our mission accomplished, we headed back to Nice.

We popped in to the hotel to store the tickets and then met up in reception again to head out. We made it as far as next door! It was a little café bar with outside tables on the street, and the very attractive landlady had asked if we wanted a beer so that was that. In fact, that was pretty much to be us for three days. The large cans and bottles of beer we were drinking were around £2 but as we kept drinking her fridge dry and she had to go to the supermarket to buy more the price started dropping. In the end we were getting them for £1. I think she was probably getting them in bulk for 50p.

The Harrogate bus was meant to be arriving in Nice by the middle of Monday afternoon. However, the suspension had given way at Calais under the weight of the beer loaded aboard. So it was early evening before it arrived. Chairman Charley came and joined our little gang as he seemed to have somehow fallen out with the whole Harrogate bus, who were glad to be rid of him. We finally left our drinking spot to go for a little wander (well, a big pub crawl) around the town. For us it was a relatively incident-free evening although we had heard stories of Leeds fans experiencing some issues with the local Arabs.

There was one debate about an African person who was clearly touting for business on the streets. Half of the group thought it could be a bloke due to the boat race on it and half due to the body and dress with gaping holes felt there was enough evidence to go with a vote of woman. Nobody was going to go close enough to do the hand test as it was scary-looking whichever way the vote went.

On matchday, we agreed after breakfast that we would make the long trip to our new local to see our landlady friend. Our little gang grew as we were joined at our street tables by three lads from Keighley. We again drank the fridge dry on a couple of occasions, meaning she had to jump in to her Renault 5 and do a mercy dash to restock. After each trip to the supermarket the beer prices seemed to go down and another button on her blouse was undone. We feel this was a ploy to keep us at her bar and it seemed to work! We swapped tales of Leeds games gone by and drank and had a right old laugh. You would have thought we had all known each other for years, not just met up.

The Keighley lads, it turned out, had been involved in one of the incidents with the Arabs the night before and had ended up in the local police station cells for the night before being let out without any charges. They were telling us about a bit of a street battle with the Arabs and one of them had grabbed a tennis racket from a basket outside a shop. Not as daft as it seems if the opposition are throwing things at you and you have a good backhand and can whack the missiles back with grace.

When they were in the cells, two of them were put in together, but the other lad was in a cell on his own with a group of mainly Arabs. They had an idea to make him safer – they would make him seem like a hard man, and the two who were together decided to invent for him a tough nickname.

They were shouting, 'Pitbull, how are you doing, mate?' 'Pitbull, keep calm, do not be kicking off, mate, we want to get out of here not get another night in the cells. Keep cool, Pitbull.'

Another little exchange involved Blockhead telling everyone about his experience around financial services and a specific credit card. He could

Jonathan Walker, Sgt Barraclough and Dave Bradley.

not remember the name of the card. One of the Bristol lads said, 'Cirrus?' to which Blockhead replied, 'Serious? Yes of course I am fucking serious! Do you think I am making this up!'

As we sat at the tables a few feet from the main road just down from the station a strange sight was to be seen on several occasions. A local police car drove past us. The coppers seemed to be moonlighting as tourists! There was a little fat guy in a Hawaiian shirt leaning out of the window and filming the local sights, which seemed to be mainly us when they went past. On the fourth pass-by someone said, 'That is not a tourist, that's Barraclough. Bloody hell, it is!' Sgt Barraclough was heading up the police intelligence unit and had decided that the south of France deserved his full **Magnum** outfit. He really was a sight to behold (more of that later).

Late afternoon, we decided it was time to head for Monaco again and we went to the train station. We had thought about the helicopter option, but it was slightly out of our price range and we would have needed to book in advance too.

When we boarded the train, it was standing room only. The Leeds fans travelling to the match were on the Paris to Monaco leg of their journey. There was a bit of an incident when some knob decided that the Bristol lads, being southerners, were not 'proper' Leeds fans. Being a shrinking violet, I said, 'I have been drinking with them for two days and I bet they have done more games than you have, mate! I've never seen you before!' It deflected attention away from them and the tension was soon defused. Maybe Crocodile Dundee stroking his weapon behind me helped, but Blockhead seemed to do that all the time anyway. Maybe he was just continually adjusting his bollocks.

When we got to Monaco we headed to a square in the centre where they were serving points all over knocking out beer for £2.50 a pint. After the beers it was time to head up to the ground, where it was clear that Monaco as a club were not used to lots of pissed fans descending upon them. The ground was more like a posh hotel with glass windows everywhere.

As we tried to get into the Leeds end there was a big queue and an almighty crush. There were crash barriers in place trying to keep people back and slow the entry. As kick-off got nearer and more and more were arriving the crush got worse and quite dangerous. There were women and a few kids in danger of getting hurt. There were not too many police around outside but those present were doing their best to try to encourage folk to move back.

You experience some crazy things at matches and what happened next was up there with them. One of the French police was holding the crowd back with his rifle across his chest and he was desperately trying to prevent the crash barriers going over and a serious incident occurring. As the crowd moved forward and I got close to him, from behind me someone took a big swing at the copper, and thankfully the punch missed.

I was not happy and told the guy on the way into the ground. He said the French police had been a right set of bastards when he had been to France with England. I said that he was helping and stopping folk getting hurt. The lad apologised and we moved on.

In the ground, Charley and I met up with an old friend from previous pre-season trips to Ireland, one of the Moran twins. It seemed there had been an incident involving him and his brother (the two are identical) and one of the other Leeds lads. As we stood chatting to him behind the goal the other lad in question turned up with a bloodied nose and quite a large group behind him. 'It is not me you want,' says the twin. 'It was my brother who chinned you.' I have known them a long time and spent a week with them in Ireland pre-season and I still struggle to tell the difference between them. It was funny to see the puzzled look on the face of the bloke thinking if it was him or not

'You best take it up with our lad, but you will get another one if you come any nearer,' said Twinny. A few comments were made about the need for the backup, but it was all smoothed over and peace and harmony happily seemed to break out. At least while we were there anyway.

The game was clearly one of our memorable away nights in Europe with a Tony Yeboah hat-trick, but almost as memorable for me was the whole Leeds end of 3,000 singing to the little fat guy in a Hawaiian shirt, to the theme of **Hawaii Five-O**, 'Ba ba ba ba Bara Baraclough, Ba ba ba ba Bara Baraclough!'

After the game there was a massive police presence to usher everyone out of town. It was a party atmosphere, but the faces of the police seemed disappointed with this. I was at the back of a sort of escort and there were police with guns and tear gas. As there were far too many to get on the first trains we broke out of the escort and went for another pint. We met a Czech Leeds fan in a bar and there was a rumour we had drawn a Czech team in the next round. This was to turn out to be false as it ended up being Eindhoven.

A Moranm but which one?

More beers were consumed in Nice to celebrate our brilliant victory, then we had a couple of drinks in the local before we did the train journey in reverse. The Bristol lads were with us until London, before Blockhead and I said our goodbyes and continued onwards to Leeds. I think a few bottles of port were consumed between Paris and Leeds.

From a bad start being kicked off my own bus, it (for me) was a better trip flying solo and meeting new Leeds fans along the way.

Eindhoven, 1995

Next up in the UEFA Cup was a trip to Holland to play PSV Eindhoven on Tuesday, 31 October.

We were 5-3 down from the home leg, which was notable for the crazy synchronised chants and movements in the cheese wedge from the travelling PSV fans.

Again, ignoring the advice/demands to go on the club trip straight there and back whilst paying through the nose, I decided along with Paul McManus (Stella) that our own road trip was our best option so we agreed to make our own way there and almost back too. There were all sorts of warnings that Leeds fans without tickets would be deported and nobody would get into the ground without a ticket but we decided we would take our chances.

The departure point for the trip was East Keswick, where I was playing football that Sunday morning. Stella was driving and picked me up at the end of the game and then drove down to London, where we had booked a train and ferry.

The ferry was an overnight sailing and we just had seats, with no accommodation booked. As it turned out we thought it was a good idea to keep drinking in the bar until they would not serve anymore and then fall asleep on the seats in the bar area anyway.

Arriving at Rotterdam early in the morning we caught a train to Eindhoven. Clearly being an athlete not used to this level of Sunday drinking, I was still drunk from the session on the ferry. Stella saved my life by grabbing my collar when I was looking the wrong way up the road and was planning on doing a Boycey (as it is known), when I nearly stepped out in front of oncoming traffic.

Having narrowly avoided death, we found a tourist information place and tried to find some accommodation for the stay. Town was quite busy so we had to settle for a hotel on the edge of town. Wanting to get the present buying out of the way and knowing it may come in useful if required to obtain a ticket, I bought an Eindhoven baseball cap from a shop. We then jumped on the bus to check in to the hotel. As we arrived, there was a welcome committee as well as the hotel reception staff, and we were greeted by two Dutch police in the reception.

'You are here for the football, you have tickets?' one of them said.

'Football, what football, who's playing?' I replied.

'No, you are here for the football,' said the cop.

'Not us, mate, we are here to see the tulips, maybe take in a flower show. Out of interest when is this game and what time in case we change our mind and might like to go?' I said, sarcastically.

The cops gave us some advice: stay away from the ground. Any Leeds supporters without a ticket would be deported.

'As we said, we are not here to watch the football, but thank you for the advice about where to avoid,' I said.

We checked in and the police, knowing they would not get a sensible answer, lost interest, shook their heads and left us alone.

After putting the bags in the room, we headed down to the ground to see what the chances were of getting a ticket. We noticed already that some of the streets leading to the ground had barriers ready to be closed off. There was clearly going to be a big security operation.

As it turned out, the chances of obtaining a ticket for the Eindhoven end looked quite slim. In the ticket office you had to show a Dutch passport and prove your name and address. Hanging around outside the ground, we bumped into a few characters from the Monaco trip, including Blockhead and a few other groups of Leeds fans.

Another familiar face then appeared – a little fat bloke in jeans and a tight fighting leather jacket. He was flanked by two much younger and taller guys who were dressed in the same outfit; it was the tight jeans and leather jacket look. It was of course Sgt Barraclough. Blockhead says, 'Where did you pick these two up, an Amsterdam gay bar?' Barraclough had clearly got himself in character dress for Holland and now just needed some clogs.

Barraclough proceeded to tell us that we should all go to Amsterdam, that everything in Eindhoven would be closed in the town centre and if we did not have tickets the best option was to stay in Amsterdam and watch on the game on the TV. He also told us there were far more Leeds out and about in Amsterdam than in Eindhoven. We are fans of doing the opposite that the plod ask that you do so we were always definitely going to stay in Eindhoven. Blockhead and quite a few shipped out to Amsterdam to hook up with the Leeds fans no doubt.

As I could not be trusted to cross the road without assistance I was not allowed to look after foreign money. Stella had the cash in a brown envelope and was buying the beer with 'our' money. We managed to find a few bars open on the Monday in the town and had a few drinks in the afternoon. We ended up in a bar where we got talking to 'Skippy', the Dutch-Australian barman. He said he would open on match night and put the game on for us if we could not get a ticket. He also decided that as he ended his shift at tea time it would be a good idea for him to come out with us and show us the sights of Eindhoven. Many more pints were sunk that day and by late evening they had sunk Stella, who dropped his second full pint in quick succession and then decided he would head back to the hotel for some sleep. He handed the brown envelope with the joint funds in over to me.

I stayed out with Skippy (actual name Jimmy) as the night was just young. Skippy decided to show me some of the more exotic pubs and clubs of Eindhoven, which seemed to be off the beaten track. The fog was like pea soup. After a few hours of drinking and watching the entertainment, not having a clue where I was, I decided my race was run too and would get a taxi back to the hotel. As the taxi driver dropped me off, I threw a handful of coins from out of the brown envelope and my pocket on to the car seat as a tip. The driver seemed happy and drove off.

I staggered to the room up the stairs, knocking loudly on the door and getting no answer. After hammering on the door a few more times and still with no answer, I started banging on the window. The curtains parted and the face of a big bloke with a bushy beard appeared. Oh shit, sorry, mate, wrong floor! Heading this time to the right floor I decided to go in reverse order and started banging hard on the window. Stella appeared at the door, and said, 'The door is open you absolute fuckwit!'

On matchday, with stories of checks on the home end for all fans entering the ground and tight security, it seemed they were expecting up to 1,000 supporters like us without tickets. We headed in to town thinking that the worse-case scenario was that we would be taking up Skippy on his kind offer to watch the game in his bar later that evening.

Discussing the events (well not all of them), of the previous evening with Stella, he was checking our money in the brown envelope. The bonus was that I had miraculously managed to return with it and still with some money in it. Stella says, 'Blimey, you and Skippy must have had a good night after I left, you have put a right dent in this.' When I said I got a taxi back in the fog and threw the loose change on the seat after paying with a note for the fare, Stella was not happy. 'You really are a fuckwit, some of those coins are £5 coins!' That is the problem if you do not let the kids look after their own money on holiday – they have no appreciation of the value of the coins. Stella enquired about the type of establishments Skippy had taken me to, implying that was probably where I really spent the coins. I just said, 'Well I made sure you had a very good night with your half of the money. I was good with my half.'

It was like being lost in the fog in a hole with an owl. Stella shrugged his shoulders and we set off to the town centre.

As expected there was a large police presence in the town, and most of the bars were indeed closed. We were talking to a couple of Leeds fans in the centre when a Dutch guy passing asked if we were looking for an open pub. Do bears shit in the woods?! We then followed him on a walk for ten minutes into a housing estate. We came to a proper, traditional pub. It was spot on and we spent quite a few hours in there.

I'm not sure if it was the extra-strength Bok beer that we were drinking but the pool table was confusing as it had no pockets, although at least you got value for money. There were quite a few Leeds fans in there and notably a lad from Whitby with one leg. The Bok beer was going down well and we were having a right laugh. The Whitby lad (Peg Leg) joked that as I had lost my Eindhoven baseball cap the night before, he had seen it in an establishment of disrepute. He said, 'I am sure I placed mine on top of an Eindhoven cap on a bedside table when I went in the back room.'

As the day wore on, we decided to move on as there were rumours circulating of some pubs now being opened for the official trips so they could get a beer. Many fans had been forced to go on the club trip as they saw it as the only way to guarantee getting in for the match.

We first popped for a pint in Skippy's bar and arranged to go back either to watch the game, or, if we got in, afterwards. As we wandered along, we bumped into a guy who asked if we wanted tickets. They were £50 each and for the Eindhoven end. It turned out that the advice to go to Amsterdam for those who had followed it was a big error. About 400 had gone on the train in the afternoon but the police were waiting at Eindhoven station for them. They were instantly all rounded up on the platform, detained and were then sent back to Amsterdam. We met one lad later, who travelled with Kippax branch and had managed to get out of the station as an old lady needed help off the train and he walked with her right past all the police. Kindness is always rewarded.

With our tickets secured, we now just needed more beer and a strategy to get in the ground. But first more beer. We found a bar where a group of Leeds fans were drinking. There was a group of about 50 or so Dutch youngsters just down the road. They looked like they had just left school, they were staying a distance away and I think just wanted to see the English fans (hooligans in their mind). We had a couple of beers when next thing Sgt Barraclough came into the pub with his two leather-clad boyfriends. 'Right lads,' he says, 'the Dutch are here and congregating we need to charge them to disperse them.' Everyone laughed. 'We need to disperse these Eindhoven fans before it gets out of hand, come on lads, we will charge them.' Everyone laughed and said, 'It is a bunch of kids, they are not a threat to anyone.' Everyone ignored him and just carried on drinking.

We needed more beer after another Barraclough comedy moment, so we made our way to another bar. We bumped into a couple of Leeds fans from Southport. One of them travelled to the cricket Tests as part of the Barmy Army. We were very, very, drunk but in need of a strategy to get in to the ground so I was planning it on the hoof. It basically involved not being able to speak so they could not tell that we were English. 'What are you going to do then, pretend to be deaf and mute?' says Stella. No, I had a cunning plan and its simplicity was brilliant. We are to buy two Eindhoven scarfs and wrap these around our faces like a mask to cover our mouths. If they ask us to remove them or start to speak to us, we quickly start to eat so they cannot understand what we are saying. We just need to buy either a sandwich or a big baguette will do. Baldrick would have been proud. After the event we discovered the two lads were writers for **The Square Ball** and my strategy made it into one of their articles about their trip to the game.

We headed off to enact the plan, taking a taxi to the ground. As we got out (fell out) of the taxi near the ground there were a couple of very attractive Dutch ladies walking towards the game.

'Would you like to escort us into the ground, ladies?'

'Piss off, you English bastards.'

'Oh, okay, I guess we could just go for a drink later then!'

'Rouse pack it in we are meant to be undercover!' says Stella.

Back to the plan and as we got outside the ground and needed to go to the souvenir shop to purchase the scarves, Stella seemed to suffer a complete loss of a sense of direction. He marched straight past the shop – which we had been to on the Monday morning – and down the side of the ground. He then heads through a door akin to the old players' entrance in the West Stand at Elland Road. I am following behind and trying to catch him up. God knows where the security guy was. Anyway, Stella is on a mission and charges up the stairs and along another corridor, as I am just about reaching. He has reached two wooden double doors and a bloke comes out and says, 'Can I help you?'

'I'm looking for the souvenir shop.'

'This is the boardroom; the shop is outside the ground.'

'Oh, sorry thanks for your help.'

'Stella, what are you doing we are meant to be undercover! We are in their West Stand!'

'I'm lost!'

'You don't say! For fuck's sake follow me.'

We leave the directors' area and go back to the souvenir shop. Stella's next job is to buy the two scarves. He is in the queue and I am stood back watching. As he gets to the front, I think two young locals have worked out we are English and when he puts his arm out to pick up a scarf the kid next to him stops him by grabbing his arm and doing a karate chop motion. Stella comes back and says he can't get any. I ask why, and he says they will not let him. I tell him to leave it to me. I walk up, tap the lad on shoulder, and say, 'I am going to buy two scarves; it would not be a good idea to touch me.' I hope it was the same lad or it would have been a bit of a strange comment in a souvenir shop. He had a very good grasp of English like all the Dutch, so we get the scarves and off we go.

As we get to the end of the ground that we are to go in there are large queues as they are indeed checking everyone's tickets and bags and talking to them. 'Okay, Stella, here we go, wrap the scarf round your face and sandwiches set to stun.'

I walk towards the steward first, ticket held up and scarf wrapped round my face. He unravels the scarf, looks at me and wraps it back up. There are some benefits of being ugly. Stella is also through with not much hassle. Thinking that's it, job's a good one, we go up the stairs to find our seats. There are two coppers on each entrance, clearly still looking for Leeds fans in their end. We pass them, get to our row and would you believe it there are four lads sat in our seats. We wave our tickets at them, trying not to speak and alert the plod. Thankfully the folk on the row behind intervened and they were sent packing without too much fuss.

Leeds were totally outplayed in the first leg and lost 5-3. We were not hopeful of a good outcome and we were proved right. The only way we gave ourselves away in the ground was not leaping up to celebrate and instead sitting laughing as John Pemberton volleyed into his own net from 30 yards out. We lost 3-0 and with the game over we headed back to Skippy's bar.

Skippy was very pleased to see us and we had a couple of pints. There were not too many people left and as the bar quietened down and we were having a natter with him, he said, 'Right, lads, you are now going to experience a traditional Dutch lock-in.'

He ushered the few stragglers out of the door, put up the closed sign and pulled down the shutters.

A traditional Dutch lock-in was basically to do the full line of optics. This is where Stella came into his element, whilst I had him dropping pints by the end of Monday after a night and a day on the beer. He is a spirit drinker, which I am not. I can drink Bacardi until it comes out

The Eindhoven scarf this year.

of my ears but other types not so much. Anyway, our Dutch-Australian friend did not want any cash – it all seemed to be on the house. It looked like the longest spirit line in the world. When we were only halfway along, I knew I was in trouble and I think I sneaked off to spew. There was a routine; it was basically pour it, drink it, pour it, drink it, repeat. I was rapidly descending on to automatic pilot. Stella again had to save my life as about three quarters of the way along it was time for the Flaming Sambuca! I had just picked it up and was ready to down it. When I say ready that probably involved picking my head up off the bar.

'Blow the thing out first for Christ sake you'll wipe the bar out if you go boom!' says Stella.

Who knows what time we finished drinking, but our train back to the ferry was at 7.45am the next day. We said our farewell to Skippy and decided to walk back to the hotel to get fresh air, although it was miles. We went to bed, which was a disaster the next morning despite setting alarms we overslept. We got dressed and tried to see if we could get a bus to get us to the train in time but there did not seem to be any around.

As we were stood at the side of the road, I noticed a Weetabix-like substance on Stella's famous leather jacket. I then remembered staggering behind him spewing for England on the walk home. I think I had spewed through my hands and it went on to his shoulder and arm. I said, 'I think you need to clean your jacket, mate.' 'For fuck's sake,' he says, 'what is that?' And then he saw me laughing. 'Its spew isn't it?' 'Well, you should not get me on that many spirits after three days on the beer.'

Despite our best efforts, which were poor given the state we were in, we missed the train and the ferry so we decided we would pay £100 and fly back to London. On the flight we met a guy who had been working with Universal Football Tours. He was not the same lad we had bought the tickets off, but he had been working on their trip. He was from Sheffield and asked if he could have a lift back up the M1. As we got to the car this proved very useful as Stella says, 'Actually, I am not fit to drive, do you fancy doing it?' 'Me?' I said. 'No not you! Fuckwit!' he replied. So our guest drove the car to Sheffield to give Stella more chance to recover.

I am convinced I had alcohol poisoning or as close as you could get to it. I felt dreadful all week. I could not drink at all, and could not even think about it without feeling ill. I drove to Thirsk from York (where I was living) on Saturday lunchtime to meet Harrogate Whites for the trip to the Riverside on Saturday, 4 November 1995. My first drink was a shandy! I still could not face alcohol. It was a little lively outside the ground after the game. I felt so fragile that I could not have taken a blow to the head. The game ended 1-1 with Brian Deane scoring.

When I got back home that night, I had an event that suited how lively I felt. A group of us went to see Val Doonican live at the York Barbican. After the show, which was very good, I did not go to the pub for a drink with the rest of them but went home as I needed more sleep before Sunday morning football. I think I then just about managed a couple of pints after playing.

5

Maritimo, 1998

Three years had passed but we were back in Europe again. When the draw was made I thought, 'Great a Portuguese side,' as I had never been to mainland Portugal. Then when I found out where Maritimo played. Where the hell is that? It is on an island made of cake in the Atlantic in a town that could just as easily have been called Fuckall.

I researched all the options and the best option we had at an affordable price and without going with the club was to do a flight from London. The only flights out were on a Saturday and the return was the following Friday, so it meant a long holiday on the granny island of Madeira in the capital, Funchal.

The travelling contingent with me for this trip was Stephen 'Toby' Westoby and 'Porno' Roy Flynn.

We flew out whilst Leeds were playing their game away at Spurs. Funchal has one of those airports where they land on a short runway, flying in over the mountains. Following an exciting landing we headed in to Funchal and looked to find some accommodation with not having booked anything in advance.

In the end we found a bed and breakfast that could take three in a room, although one of us would have to sleep on a mattress on the floor. We got the room for about £8 each a night. In deciding who would sleep on the mattress I decided that as I was the organiser, I should take control. 'Toby, your nickname was a dog in **The Wizard of Oz**, therefore, it is only fair that you kip on the floor.' 'Sounds okay with me,' he says.

Having checked in we headed out to explore. Leaving the gaff was very interesting as it was basically a door out on to the main road that ran past the hotel but there was no path and usually the cars and motorbikes were flying past like maniacs. It was bad enough sober and we consoled ourselves that the road would be quiet when we were coming back in the middle of the night.

We headed out and had a few pints on the sea front, then stumbled across a bar that was like a traditional British pub. We called the pub The Scum Lion, although the name of the place was really The Red Lion. There were a few small groups of Leeds fans around who had done the same as us and travelled out, missing the Spurs game. We had a decent Saturday night session in the pub. There was a lad from Darlington (looked a bit like Gazza) telling us about smuggling trips to Andorra. He was offering up some fake coins and notes for folk to buy at a reasonable cost. In the end there might have been about 20 or so Leeds in the pub which was to become our local.

Later that night, Stan Julien walked in. Stan was now head of the police intelligence unit following Barraclough's retirement. Stan was dressed in a very sharp silver suit. We had thought he was a Hot Chocolate tribute act when he first walked in. He said hello and just had a drink at the bar. One of the lads in the bar said, 'He's on his own; this is the best chance we'll ever have to do him in.'

Now call me picky but assaulting a copper (hold that thought) on an island with one flight on and off a week did not strike me as possibly the best move you could ever make. I do not think there were many backers for his plan, and we carried on drinking and Stan drank up and left.

Day one over, we headed back to the bed and breakfast and on Sunday morning we were nursing our hangovers. Toby was complaining that as the windows were open and there were flower boxes on the window ledges, he reckoned he was getting mozzies attacking him. When we eventually got up there was a rota system for the bathroom. Toby was adamant he was having a bath, so Roy went first, then me and then finally it was Toby's turn.

Toby had given the game away that he wanted a nice bath. Being a wind-up merchant, I came up with a little plan to hide the bath plug. I put the sink plug in the bath as it was about half the size of the hole and hid the bath plug inside the toilet roll tube.

Toby went into the bathroom and started asking where the bath plug was. I said it was there when I had one earlier. I was waiting for him to come out and I was going to 'fess up and tell him where it was but heard water running and he was in there for ages so I thought he must have found it. When he came out, he was moaning like hell, 'That bath is shite! the plug is only half the size of the hole, I have had to keep the tap running and put my foot over the hole to try and keep any water in the bath.' 'You should have said, we could have asked at reception if they had one,' I said. With the frivolity over we decided to head out.

We walked up the hill from the town to an area where most of the larger tourist hotels seemed to be and we found a decent hotel with a pool bar. We had a few pints and used the pool area.

That evening we followed our same routine sea front bars until the sun had gone down. We saw a few more groups of Leeds down there including James Brown and Scunny (Dr Who). We then headed via a couple more bars on the way to The Scum (Red) Lion.

A little fella in the bar, one of the locals, struck up conversation with us. He looked like Tattoo from **Fantasy Island**. He told us he had a club, and that if we wanted to go there he was happy to invite us. We agreed that on the Monday night we might take him up on his offer. After another long session we returned to our hotel.

Monday followed the same routine. We got up and headed for the hotel with the pool. Now one of our party, Porno Roy, while we were having some nice lunchtime and afternoon pints in the sun, decided to tell us he was not happy (not that he ever is).

Roy said, 'I don't like drinking using facilities somewhere I am not a resident.'

I told him, 'Roy, they aren't that busy and they are happy to take our money. Shut up and drink.'

Well, he carried on bleating about it on and off all day and night.

We did the regular sea front pub crawl and worked our way to The Scum Lion. We had a big session in there and agreed with Tattoo that we would go to his club another night as we'd had a few days on the beer and would try save ourselves for matchday. All the way home Roy was still going on about his desire to move to a hotel with a pool. We ended up somehow stumbling on another bar and having another hour or so on the beer before heading back to the hotel.

On the Tuesday, Roy and Toby were awake before me and woke me up. 'Get up, Dave, we are going to go find a hotel to book with a pool.' 'Look, I have told you I am happy here and walking to the pool we have been using. If you want to move go find it book it and I will get up and come with you then. I am staying in bed and not moving until I have to.' They disappeared off to return just over hour later.

'Right get up and pack we have booked a hotel with a pool,' they said. I asked where. 'You will see,' they said. We left and headed up the hill towards the tourist hotels. They turned in to the hotel we had been using. 'You are having a laugh, aren't you?' 'No, we have booked five nights in here in a triple room.' 'How much?' I asked. They said it was £27 a night. 'That is not bad; you have done well.' Then they tell me that is £27 a night each.

Having had a right old moan about how Roy had put £100 dent in my drinking fund we checked in and dropped things in the room. We went by the pool for a while and then we had a few at the sea front before returning to get changed for the match. I was sat in reception with Toby waiting for Roy to finish his shower and get ready. Woxy from Harrogate and his then other half Leslie walked in. We agreed to wait for them before heading out. Woxy came down first for a beer while Lesley got ready. Woxy says, She has had a right go at me! She thinks I have arranged to meet you three here all along and it has been a stitch-up.' 'Just blame Roy,' I said, 'I was happy at the £8 gaff. You have caused more trouble, Roy!'

Lesley arrived and we went out for pre-match beers. The game itself was not the best. We lost 1-0 on a poor pitch having won 1-0 at home. There had been more action in the away end than on the pitch with a few small groups of Leeds fans clearly having fallen out and chasing each other around. To be fair, it seemed a far better idea having a game of tig than watching the poor game. In extra time there was no change to the score before we romped penalties, winning 4-1, and the players tried to climb in the away end. There had generally been a bad atmosphere hanging over the game due to the departure of George Graham and uncertainty as to what would be happening. Anyway, that's quite enough football.

Walking away from the ground, I remember a local was impressing everyone with an exhibition of his martial arts skills, on his own stood on a bridge. Impressive high kicks and everything with the invisible man. Everyone just shrugged and walked past him. We regrouped and headed to The Scum Lion. A few Leeds fans were in there and Tattoo was also in residence sat in his usual seat at the end of the bar. After a few beers and a natter with Tattoo he said that he needed to go to his club but insisted that the three of us head down and he would get us a beer. He gave us a card with the directions on and we said we would be down there in an hour or so.

What was Tattoo's club? Was it the local social/working men's club? Much to our delight, it turned out to be the main strip joint in Funchal. Seeing us walk in (there were no bouncers on the door), Tattoo called us over and he got a champagne bucket provided for us at the bar.

We drank free champagne, chatted with Tattoo, watched beautiful women stripping on the main stage and had plenty of them drinking with us around the bar. Most of the girls were from Brazil and it seemed they

Mark (Woxy) Wilson leading the singing at his 60th.

got a boat to Madeira then worked there to earn money for the next leg of the journey to mainland Europe. The club was very modern and impressive in its décor. We must have been there quite a while and been on our third free bucket of champagne when Roy came up to me and said, 'Dave, we're off in a few minutes. Toby wants to go back to the hotel.'

I looked at Toby laughing, talking to Tattoo surrounded by attractive girls and quaffing the free glasses of champagne whilst a pretty blonde was performing on the main stage. I thought that this looked like just the sort of place Toby would leave in a hurry.

Half hour later Toby came up to me and said, 'It's great in here! Why do you want to leave?'

'Me? I do not want to leave!'

Toby then says, 'Roy told me you wanted to leave.'

After laughing, we both turned to Roy and said, 'Roy, if you want to go back you go back, we are staying.'

A few minutes later, Roy departed back to the hotel. He had now earned his other nickname with the lads, Pleasure Dodger! It could not have been more apt.

After the free drinks had been exhausted, we had to start buying our own. I was talking to a young, dark-haired, very attractive Brazilian lass whilst Toby seemed to have gone for a doppelgänger of his wife, in the guise of a 38-year-old Brazilian who had three kids.

It became clear that as well as the drinks no longer being free the girls were also wanting to move things to a more commercial arrangement. It was obvious that they were making their money from disappearing into a back room with some of the visitors to the club.

I was on the dancefloor with my young lady. Although her English was not great, I thought we were getting by. I thought she had been trying to negotiate at one point when she was saying something about '23 anos'. We were on the dance floor for a while and she was doing her best to tempt me to go with her behind the curtains. After a while it became clear that she was not going to be dancing anymore. She seemed to want £100 for me to pay a visit with her. I said whilst I was happy to dance, I was not paying for sex. She asked, 'How much do people pay for sex with girls in Leeds?' and when I said, 'Down Holbeck heard you can get it for £10,' she flipped, ranted, and stormed off angrily into the back room on her own. To be fair I did not blame her, she was a very attractive young lady and I imagine she took £10 as more than a bit of an insult.

I went to drink my beer over where Toby was sat chatting to his 'new' wife. He had progressed from free champagne to passing his card behind the bar and paying £90 for a large bottle of the stuff. As we were talking, a tall woman in a very tight mini skirt, crop top and with the flattest chest you have ever seen wandered over. It turns out she was the head boss lady of the girls. She started dancing up to me and twice tried to shove her hand down my shorts. Toby and his lady friend were laughing uncontrollably. I thought they knew something I did not. I looked at the flat chest and chiselled face. I said, 'You're not a bloke, are you? You've got hands like a goalkeeper.' I decided it was my turn to shove my hands down and thankfully the male sex test was negative. God knows why I did that and what I would have done if it was not a woman.

We had a few more beers and Toby was getting on very well with wifey. I had got rid of the boss lady. We decided it was time to go and Toby was asking wifey out on a proper date the following night. They agreed to meet at 7.30pm and he gave her the hotel details where we were staying just in case.

We got back to the hotel and it was about 5am. We had only been in bed about an hour when the telephone rang. Roy answered the phone and I heard him go, 'No, no, no there is not a Mr Stevens here.'

Who was that, Roy? He says, 'It was reception trying to put a woman through for a Mr Stevens.' I said, 'Roy, Toby's name is Stephen Westoby, it will have been his lady that he met last night.'

Wednesday morning and Toby was not happy at the incident with Roy and the potential missed call. We hung out around the hotel in the morning. We decided we would stop off the beer for a while and Toby and myself decided to play snooker in the hotel in the afternoon. Roy had decided to do a tourist walk in the countryside with Woxy and Leslie.

Me and Toby watched a film in the room whilst we waited for them to return. It was **Harry's Game** (no, not Harry Redknapp's life story, it was a film about a British agent undercover hunting an IRA assassin).

When they returned, we got ready and headed out for a few beers. Lesley was staying in. We were amused by the stories of the walk they had done which basically involved being a mountain goat. They walked in the hills along a cliff ledge and the path got really narrow with a drop of hundreds of feet if you got it wrong. They did not have proper walking gear and given Roy has fallen off a roof and damaged his back before, it did not seem like the best of ideas.

We were having a beer at a location where Toby thought he might have been meant to meet his date but there was no sign of her. However, a Norwegian guy who was about 60 turned up with a couple of young blondes. We were sat outside, and he came and sat at the table next to us. Toby struck up a conversation with them and a little bit of banter was flying around. After about half an hour the bloke, out of the blue, offered Toby the chance to accompany him to their apartment and join in some afternoon delight. Toby declined and then spent the next hour beating himself up for not taking him up on the invite.

'Do you think it is a mistake? Do you think I should have gone with them?' he asks.

'Well, they were very attractive. What is the worst that could have happened?'

We then remind him of the tale of the lad from Knaresborough who went with a prostitute, then when she handcuffed him, a bloke jumped out of the cupboard and bummed him.

Urban myth or fact, Toby decided it was not a scene he wanted to be part of!

Quite perplexed by these events and this offer on the granny island we had a few beers at a few more bars and of course ended up in The Scum Lion. There were four other Leeds fans there so we were having a good old natter about what it meant to people to follow Leeds, how long they had been going etc. As the stories flowed as well as the beer, Toby came out with a poignant profound quote when he announced to the group, 'We're not Leeds, We ARE Leeds.'

Toby spouts some incoherent mixed-up bollocks at times (all the time really) but in context of the conversation we were having it seemed that everyone that night understood what he meant from the passion and tone of his voice when he said it. You had to be there, but it was a statement that truly summed up how we all felt about following Leeds. How it truly felt to be a Leeds fan amongst the Leeds family at some far-flung away game in Europe.

Woxy and Roy decided they were going back to the hotel. Toby and I decided to return to Tattoo's club. When we got there, I noticed that

Very profound – Toby.

Toby's new Mrs was in the company of a Middle Eastern-looking chap. Toby was not looking best pleased. I decided I would do the decent thing and went over to talk to the guy.

'Do you speak English?' 'Yes,' he replies. 'There are a lot of lovely ladies in this club my friend wants to talk to this lady so it would be really nice and good if you could find another lady to talk to.'

He basically told me no. 'Well, I have tried to warn you, my friend will not like it and I have asked you nicely and tried to help you. Don't complain to me about your nose.' 'My nose, why would I complain about my nose?' 'When he rearranges it for you with his forehead,' I said to him.

Tattoo called us over and wanted a word and to give us another set of free beers. A girl turned up with a bruise on her face. It turned out that after we had left the night before, four Cockneys had gone to the club and things got a bit out of hand. They never had trouble and therefore generally had no need for bouncers. One of the men, who had been very drunk, had slapped the girl. We said it was out of order and wished we had still been there.

About an hour later we got our wish. Three blokes walked in and the girls said it was the Cockneys. One of them pointed out the guy who had hit the girl and we said we would encourage them to leave. Toby approached the guy and said, 'You are not welcome in here, so you best get out now.' The bloke said, 'You don't work here, it is nothing to do with you.'

I assume fuelled by watching the undercover spy film in the afternoon as well as beer, I said, 'Well we do now, we are hired security!' I grabbed the guy's collar of his jacket with one hand, jabbed two fingers in the back of his head from my other hand as if it was a gun and we both marched him outside. 'Get on your knees,' I said. I assume I was thinking of executing him with my imaginary gun. Luckily for him the worst he got was Toby putting his foot in the middle of his back and him ending up face down in the dirt. Toby said, 'Now piss off and don't come back.'

When we returned inside his two mates left without any further issue. We must have looked the part as they wandered off away from the club and we went back inside. Tattoo was very pleased, and we were treated to the usual free buckets of champagne. We had a very good night and left. I could not stop laughing about it all the way back; what the hell was I doing with a fake finger gun?

When we got back to the hotel the entrance was closed and no one was about on reception to let us in. We decided we would climb over the fence and knock on the window to get Roy to let us in. We had to walk past the pool though and as Toby was right next to the edge, well you just would! I would and I did, a slight nudge and in he went fully clothed. 'You bastard!' he shouts at me. It was like kids, he was fuming and wanted to get me back, so I saved him the bother as he chased me and I just jumped in anyway. The guy on reception who should have let us in appeared, and was not very happy. We had broken the pool curfew. We were being noisy and making the hotel floors wet. We ran to our room dripping everywhere down the corridor. When we got in the room, Roy said, 'Oh that carry on at the pool I could hear was you two idiots, I should have known.'

On Thursday, we were up a bit later after our late-night exploits at Tattoo's club and when I got to the pool Roy was in his usual place sat on a sun lounger reading his paper.

I was having my usual hangover cure dip in the pool. I was in the water hanging off the side of the pool when I started talking to Roy.

'Roy, can I ask you something?'

'Yes, what?' says Roy.

'Ever since we've been at this hotel you have never been in the pool.'

'Yes, I know, I just like sitting here reading my paper.'

'But you insisted you wanted a hotel with a pool. You could sit anywhere and read a paper. Why don't you get in the pool for a swim?'

'Oh, I can't swim,' says Roy.

'What? You had better learn fast! You are having a laugh, we have now paid £100 extra each this week for a pool for you and you can't bastard swim, for fuck's sake Roy!'

On Thursday we were in wind-down mode. A few beers were had but the local brew was becoming difficult to drink; very tinny and leaving a strange taste in the mouth. We were just about ready for home. We used the pool area a bit, played snooker and watched a couple of films. I noticed a sign on the wall that said '18 anos' next to the snooker table. I laughed.

'Oh,' I said. 'That Brazilian lass was telling me here age. I thought she was trying to agree a price when I was dancing with her and said "23 anos", it was 100 anyway.'

'She was not 100 years old,', says Toby.'If there was one 100 years old, she would have done for you, Roy.'

We headed out for a beer and bumped into Woxy, who was in a flap saying that the police were everywhere. There had been an incident the previous night. He would not stay out and went back as he genuinely thought it could be to do with us at Tattoo's club. We had a farewell drink at The Scum Lion and then a farewell visit to Tattoo's club. Another Brit in the club reckoned the Cockneys had told folk they were off-duty coppers from London. I somehow found that hard to believe, especially if he thought my fingers could be a gun to his head.

We had an early night as we had an early flight home. It had been yet another entertaining trip on the road with a little bit of football thrown in for good measure, and then we got back to see us lose at home to Leicester 1-0 on the Saturday.

Despite having a great time, we would not really recommend Madeira as a location for a group of lads. It is in the main granny island holiday destination and you can see why. Though Tattoo greeting 'di plane, di plane' for us did make it a bit of a fantasy island for a few days.

6

Roma, 1998

Next up in the European adventures was a trip to Rome. The travelling contingent for this one was 'Porno' Roy Flynn, Stephen 'Toby' Westoby, Andrew 'Boycey' Boyes, Anthony 'Ev' Everitt, Roger Allison, Nige Fawcett and his girlfriend Rachel. We travelled through the night in a couple of cars to Stansted for the flight to Rome.

Rouse Tours had booked us in to a very reasonably priced hotel. We got the train to Rome and then walked to find the hotel. To our horror it was slap bang next to a police station and from the outside the concrete walls made it look like a prison. However, when we entered the hotel it was a really nice place and staffed by a lot of very pleasant young ladies.

We soon discovered that Rome was full of café bars and the Italians loved to drink coffee and eat cake. The place was not awash with proper bars or pubs but virtually every café bar sold beer. We never seem to have a problem sniffing out a decent bar.

Over the course of the few days in Rome I continued my cultural tour of Europe by drinking in the nearest bar to the famous tourist attractions, whilst some people had a look around. On this occasion I drank outside the Vatican and the Colosseum.

On the first night, after a long day on the beer, Roy was struggling as he had driven through the previous night to get us to Stansted. Roy was very drunk and as a result he had decided he smoked. He also looked like he was about to fall asleep. We were on bottled beers and as Roy put a cigarette in his mouth, I put my bottle above his head and poured beer on the end of the cig. Roy was then trying to light the fag, and after about four goes he raised an eyebrow looked at the cigarette in his hand and threw it on the floor in disgust. He then took another out of the packet. Of course, as soon as it was in his mouth, I did the same again. His eyes were closing so much that he did not notice the beer and went through the same routine ending up with the fag on the floor. This happened about three times before I got bored and allowed him to notice what I was doing. His response rhymed with cat.

Whilst we were in the bar a very loud Japanese transvestite flounced into the place in a bright purple blouse. He said something to us at the bar and someone (I cannot remember who) said, 'We are straight but our mate over there is gay and looking for a man.' Roy was virtually asleep leaning against a pillar. Our Japanese friend flounced across and much to our amusement started to give Roy a cuddle. Roy's face was a picture as he opened his eye, then raised an eyebrow again at the sight that presented itself before him. The Japanese chap seemed to want to take it too far and usher Roy off into the night with him. We decided it was time to put an end to the joke. We told him we were joking, that Roy was not gay! The Japanese fella decided to go all drama queen and stroppy and did not want to leave it at that. We ended up having to quite forcefully tell him to do one.

Roger got very upset with us, 'You let him come over to talk to us and then you led him on. You're out of order now getting nasty to him and threatening him to make him go away.'

'Oh, sorry Roger, what do you suggest? That we let him shag Roy?'

It was another scene that Toby did not want to be a part of, so we moved on.

We were out for a long time and eventually got split up. I ended up on my own and met some Leeds fans late on in the night drinking outside some bars. They were a group of lads from down south who I have seen quite often at away games since. I amused them with renditions of 'Deidre Barlow to the IRA' and my spectacular dancing to the 'When

Roy – not sure what is occurring.

Johnny comes marching home' tune. The latter being a little ditty that a bloke with a tin whistle played as we were waiting to get let out at away games in late 1970s and early 80s. One of the lads, who I was sat next to at QPR in 2019, still calls me 'Deidre' due to that song.

After the drinking was over, I seemed to be lost so I thought I would get the tube as there was a stop near our hotel. I boarded the tube and promptly fell asleep and ended up at the end of the line, miles out of town. I got off waited five minutes and got on to go back. I only went and did the same thing again, this time ending up at the other side of town. After about three goes I thought I would walk. I seemed to walk for hours before seeing anywhere I recognised, and it still took me over an hour from then to get to the hotel. Why didn't I just ring a taxi?.

I got in about six o'clock in the morning and climbed into my bunk bed.

It turned out I was not the only one drunk and lost. In the hotel, we had a communal toilet and bathroom. Rachel had gone to the toilet in the middle of the night to be confronted by the sight of a stark-naked and drunk Toby asleep sat on the toilet. She escorted him back to his room. When she opened the door, he said, 'Look at that lot, they are pissed.' He also told us the next day that he was pretty sure she liked what she had seen, and it was a thrill for her.

On matchday, we had a day in the café bars before making our way up towards the ground. We had hours to get there but as time passed quickly in the end, we had to catch a service bus out to the ground as we were running out of time. There were a few other Leeds fans on the bus too. We got off to walk the remaining half-mile. On the walk to the ground, there were gangs of scooter boys driving up fast and close to the Leeds fans on the way to the ground. Everyone was getting wound up about this. One supporter, a big guy, pulled out a sapling tree planted in the middle of the wide footpath. When he heard the next 'hairdryer' engine behind us approaching fast, he held out the tree and blocked the route. The scooter had to swerve out of the way, nearly making its riders come off.

As we got to the ground itself we were about to walk around to the Leeds end, and there were a few fans wandering around. One young lad had his Leeds Union Jack flag stolen by an Italian, but before the thief could get far he bumped into two big lads who I recognised from York.

One of them then held his hand out and insisted the Italian gave him the flag and then handed it back to the young lad.

The Italian scooter gang had turned up and formed a semi-circle around us, maybe 20-odd bikes all with two onboard. There was a bit of a stand-off, then one of the Italians spat at Boycey. Boycey pointed his finger at the Italian and charged at him. The lad dropped his scooter then turned and ran into the car park with Boycey in hot pursuit. I told the rest of them to go to the Leeds end and that I would go and retrieve Boycey.

I found Boycey, who had not managed to catch the Italian, and told him we needed to go to get in to the ground. On our way an Italian lad on his own started talking to us. He was not like the typical Italians we had seen; he was built like a rugby player and six foot plus. He said, 'The away end is round there but do not go through the tunnel, you will get ambushed and they have knives. Walk around with me.' He took us a route around that avoided the tunnel and pointed us into the away end. We thanked him and went in. It was lucky that we met him as about five minutes after we got in the ground a group of Leeds fans came in and one of them had been slashed on the leg with a knife. A known ploy of the Italian hooligans is to stab you on the legs / buttocks. They treat it as a minor crime using a knife unless they stab you in the torso.

Leeds did well but were to lose the game 1-0. Leaving the ground, we had agreed to meet back at a bar in the town. We were walking around the streets near the ground when we thought we were going to meet some more big Italians. Two very tall people were slowly walking towards us in the dark. As they got closer, we worked out that they were not Italians, they were instead Dougie Kaye and his son Josh from Harrogate. They joined us and we met up in town with the rest of the travelling group for a few beers.

The following day, after a day seeing the tourist attractions from the comfort of nearby bars (including the Vatican and the Colosseum), we were out in Rome. Roger and Boycey had been winding each other up all day long but in the end decided they'd had enough beer and agreed to walk back to the hotel together. Toby and I ended up in a pub in the middle of town. We had walked past what was the closest to a proper pub we had seen with a group of Italian lads, maybe a dozen or so drinking in the street outside.

We had a seated area outside the bar we were in on the opposite corner of the street. We met another Leeds fan who we were having a conversation with. At this point three other Leeds fans emerged from the pub over the road and decided to come to our bar. They had a couple of pints with us but to say we did not take to them would be an understatement. We were quite pleased when they decided they were leaving. We all collectively as they left said what a pain in the arse those three were. As they walked away and turned the corner a few seconds later about eight of the Italian lads from the pub decided to follow them.

The three of us looked at each other, nodded, and got up to go follow them in case they were in trouble. Despite us not getting on with them, they were Leeds, and we were not going to let them get a kicking without helping them out.

We turned the corner of the street and the Italian lads were walking back down the road towards us. One of them shrugged his shoulders and put his arms out as if to say, 'Where did they go?' They must have legged it as soon as they turned the corner knowing they had wound the Italian lads up and that they were following them. One of the Italians touched his cap as he walked back towards the pub and we returned to our beer in the bar. It was as if the Italian lads knew what we had done but were okay with us about it.

We enjoyed the trip, although Rome seemed to consist of café bars or large Irish bars and nothing in between. We drew the home leg with Roma 0-0 and so ended the 1998 European excursions. For the team we had at the time, we had acquitted ourselves very well against a Totti-led Roma.

We were hoping we could qualify again as it had certainly whetted our appetite for more of these European trips.

7

Moscow, 1999

When the draw against Lokomotiv Moscow was revealed it was quickly apparent that this was not going to be the easiest place to get to in the world. We all agreed that we wanted to stay in Moscow for a long period of time and so we would not be going on the club trip. It took a little bit of research and clarification of what would be involved. This basically meant first needing a voucher from your accommodation inviting you to stop in Moscow. When this was obtained it needed to be sent along with everyone's details to the Russian Embassy in London to obtain a travel visa.

This was going to have to be done on this occasion for a party of 15 on Rouse Tours. I had to reimburse work for a few hours spent on the fax machine to get it all sorted out. We were travelling in two groups with ten of us who were going out on the Monday and then a further five coming out on the Tuesday.

Leeds had won the first leg at Elland Road 4-1 on 21 October 1999.

We booked flights with Lufthansa from Manchester, we had our accommodation, and our visas were all sorted, so the trip could commence.

In a programme ahead of the game, a Russian Lokomotiv fan had put an item in with his e-mail address asking for people to contact him. Smithy had e-mailed him and on the night of our departure I parked my car in Leeds to travel to Manchester Airport with Smithy. We had a few hours before we needed to set off and I came up with an idea to try and wind up our travelling party, many of whom had been saying they really did not know what to expect in Russia. I decided on a plan to doctor the e-mail we had received from Alex the Russian to paint a picture of the country and our hosts to the group.

I did think in the end I had too much time and had overdone it, and it felt like it was too daft and far-fetched for them to ever fall for it. Time would tell and we would see. The English was actually very good in the e-mail, but I turned it into a version of what I thought might be a Russian trying to use pidgin English and dumbed it down considerably. I implied that there were very few women out on a night in Moscow and that the Lokomotiv fans all drank together and then went back to their bar (a place I called the Loko club) and in there they spent the night drinking and all dancing together. I also suggested that they could take us to a traditional Russian pub with a pit in the cellar and we could have a chance to wrestle with a bear. There was no risk of injury to us, though, as I said in the e-mail that all of its teeth and claws had been removed. The worst we would get was a nasty suck. There was a load of other tosh I had put in. I had printed a copy of the doctored e-mail to share with our travelling party on the journey. The real message had invited us to meet up but also to play football in a gymnasium at the side of the football ground the night before the game, which we were planning to do, so we had instructed the lads to bring some football kit to wear.

We got to Manchester and found that they had over-booked our flight so of the first wave some had to go via Paris whilst the other half went via Frankfurt. The half who had been moved to another flight were given £150 vouchers and arrived in Moscow just half an hour behind us. It still did not stop some of them having a moan about it.

When we arrived in Moscow, as we were passing through the airport I passed the e-mail around for people to read. There were a series of reactions to it, including from Will, who said, 'Who are we meeting? Are this lot gay? This says they drink all night and then dance together.' Then Chrissie latched on to the issue of animal rights and cruelty, 'What sort of a place have we come to that they still do this to animals in 1999, it is disgusting. I had not realised they were still so backward.' It had clearly been a long journey through the night and their wind-up radar was not working as they were falling for it hook, line and sinker.

We all regrouped when we had got through customs. Leaving the arrivals exit there was a bloke with a sign saying Rouse Tours on it. This was our driver. All I remember was that Moscow airport felt like the darkest place on Earth. It was cold and did not seem that welcoming.

We were transferred by minibus to our hotel in the outskirts of Moscow. The e-mail was still being passed around.

We checked in to the hotel and then all headed to the bar in the foyer. We had agreed to meet Alex, the Russian lad who had e-mailed us, in the bar. Will was still babbling on about Russians being gay. There were ex-soldiers in uniform working as security and guarding the hotel entrance doors. Locals would not normally be allowed in but as they were invited in by us to visit this rule was ignored.

Alex was younger and long-haired, while Dimitri was older and bald. This just cemented it with Will who was continually dropping daft comments to them. Me and Smithy decided it was time to come clean about the e-mail before it caused some bother. Alex read it and was bemused as he said, 'But my English is not this bad!' I think he worked out it had been a wind-up for the others and found it quite funny.

We decided to drink the vodka and treat our Russian guests, who said the price to them was expensive but to us it was very cheap. We kept ordering 'giraffes' of vodka, as we christened the large ones. We had quite a few of these over several hours and it was weird as we did not feel like we were getting drunk until we decided to go to a nearby bar. When we got outside the hotel and the fresh air hit us, everybody developed wobbly legs and was staggering around. We then managed a couple of beers in the bar before returning to the hotel. We had a couple more drinks then called it a day. We had agreed to meet up at the ground for the football and then head into Moscow with them the following night.

On the Tuesday, we all got up and despite being wasted on the Russian vodka it was very strange. We all noticed that no one had a hangover. It was as if we had not even had a drink so we decided that it was good gear with no chemicals pumped into it. We went to the restaurant to sample a Russian buffet breakfast, which was not bad although it was a bit strange that there was a carvery-style meat counter with something that must have been a fully sized deer or moose on it for you to help yourself to alongside the usual bacon and eggs.

We finished breakfast and headed in to Moscow on the underground, which was impressive with the marble walls, statues and various carvings etched in. We had a wander around and took in the sights. Moscow was a city of extremes and it seemed you were either a beggar on the streets, working in a shop, or if a bloke wandering around in gangs in leather jackets. I was shaking my head as Will had heard you could barter for things and brought a full black bin liner full of soaps and other items to negotiate with. When he opened it in the centre of Moscow it was funny as he was quickly surrounded and about 50 people dived in for his freebies. It was like he was trying to feed a group of rowdy pigeons.

We had a couple of beers and then headed back to the hotel. The other five were arriving and we needed them as for the seven-a-side match against the Russians as we only had four players present. The pre-match warm-up for the four of us involved about another four pints in the hotel whilst we waited.

The five stragglers arrived and literally had to check in, get their footie gear and head off to the stadium. We were playing in a gymnasium next to Lokomotiv Moscow's ground. When we got there we were met by Alex and Dimitri who took us into the gym. Blimey, we thought, there were about 40 of them. We had the bare seven plus a couple of spectators, the others preferring to go to the pub instead.

The gymnasium, whilst quite large, was a handball court so had goals like a hockey pitch which would work in our favour as Smithy, our keeper, virtually filled the space. They agreed that we would play teams of seven of them one after the other. I knew we were going to be up against it. There was only me and Toby who played at a decent standard regularly and we were in the twilight of our careers. We had a few Sunday league second team players, plus lads who just had a kick-about, and we had two goalkeepers playing outfield. How can you take three keepers for a seven-a-side game!.

Anyway, we did not let ourselves down and as predicted our biggest asset was our keeper Smithy who was undoubtedly player of the tournament and kept us in most matches. We played four games of 15 minutes and got a creditable set of results: 1-1, 1-0, 0-0 and finally a 2-1 defeat. The Russians said they would now play a half-hour game with their best seven players against us. We said we had played for an hour so we would have a break. We instead let them play 20 minutes between themselves before taking them up on the 30-minute challenge. We think the FA and FIFA had set the fixture list to shaft Leeds again.

Predictably they were much the fresher team and it did not help that they were very good too. They ended up beating us 4-1, which probably was not a fair reflection on their dominance, although I think we were 1-1 at half-time before some legs were going and the effects of the beer kicked in. However there was a moment near the end that will always stick in my memory. As good as Smithy had been for us, their keeper in the last minute pulled off possibly the greatest reaction save I have ever seen. The bastard had to go and do it against me!

A corner was hit to me and I made a run across the defenders and hit the ball sweetly from about four yards into the bottom corner of the goal. I was already celebrating when the keeper, who was in the middle of the goal, somehow got down and got a hand on it to push it on to the post and out. It defied the laws of physics how he could get down so low so fast. He did not speak English but we formed a connection akin to Booby Moore and Pelé as a result of that one moment of pure brilliance.

Boycey, Dave Smith, Roger Allison and Toby. Kneeling – Will Martin, Rouse and Nige Fawcett.

With the football over it was time for our Russian hosts to give us a tour of Moscow. It did not start that well as they took us into a couple of American-themed bars that had very few people in. I had a word with one or two of them and said, 'Do you normally drink in these places?' The answer was, 'No, we thought you would like these bars, it's where the tourists go.' I said, 'We want to go to the bars where you normally drink, not these, I guess the beer will be cheaper and we will be able to get more rounds of drinks in.' That worked and we were in their bars in double quick time.

Toby and Boycey around this time had become a double act, almost inseparable when out and about. They had developed the name 'the brutal bothers' for themselves and they were always getting into some scrape or other.

Toby, for some reason – probably beer – on this day out had taken to winding up Boycey, who does not need much persuading to act like a knob, so when we were walking between bars every street corner there seemed to be some incident. I was sorting Boycey out and a large Russian lad who looked like Meat out of the film **Porky's** was having to sort out whoever the local was that Boycey was locking horns with. This seemed to happen at least five times.

We ended up in a lively bar right in the middle of town. We were teaching the Lokomotiv fans, who hated Spartak, some chants. We had been singing to them 'Manchester, wank, wank, wank' and they were trying to copy it, which was very funny as their version came out as 'Spartak wink, wink, wink'.

Roy Coles, aka Collar, of Kippax fame, walked into the bar. 'What are you lot doing? You do realise Lokomotiv are like Palace in London and Spartak are the equivalent of a Tottenham or Chelsea.' We just laughed as we were not over bothered, probably due to the beer, and there was enough of us in both parties to make us a fairly big group.

We stayed in this bar a while. I was happy as it stopped the babysitting and breaking up Boycey's incidents with random Russians on street corners. I was talking to the other babysitter, Meat, at the back of the pub. He was a tall lad, maybe 6ft 4in, with dark hair and wearing a leather jacket hence the similarity with Meat. Will has always been a charmer and decided to say to the lad, 'Who do you think you are, Elvis?' His reaction was, 'Fuck off! I hate Americans.'

We then had an encounter with a very intimidating fella. We were still mainly stood at the back of the bar when this huge, bald bloke, in a full-length leather trench coat, walked to the front. He pointed, shouted something that may have been about foreigners and made an action indicating he might be able to pick someone up and break them over his knee. It felt like he was pointing right at you and I said to Meat, 'Bloody hell, are your knees knocking, mine are!' Meat says, 'No problem, I would do him easy.' I thought, brilliant I am right behind you, on you go lad. Meat was a big lad and clearly fit but this guy was nearly his size and twice as big in his build. His neck was nearly as wide as most folks' bodies. He was of the biggest and scariest blokes I have ever seen.

Toby and Boycey (Brutal brothers).

He left without doing anything and when everyone was talking about it Boycey appeared as if from nowhere. He had been in a back room where there was a bit of a dancefloor. When he heard us talking, he said, 'Who that big, bald guy? He's okay, I was trying to talk to him round there.'

Toby says, 'Boycey was pointing at him and prodding him in the chest.' Talk about having a tiger by the tail, but it was no wonder he hated foreigners meeting Boycey.

Having re-joined the group, Toby and Boycey were getting dafter. They seemed intent on causing an incident with someone. Some of the others had gone back and a few of the Russians were heading off home, so I said to Toby and Boycey, 'Smithy and me are off, we are going to see if we can find a club.' They were happy enough, so we left them with a couple of the Russians and headed off.

We had not gone far when there was an alleyway that you could hear the strains of music emerging from. 'Shall we go in here,' I said. 'Not sure about it,' says Smithy. We walk down the alley and there is a group of about 15 big guys stood near the entrance. Smithy goes, 'Not sure we should be going in here.' 'What is up? They are just bouncers, we have them in England too, we are off in!' I said.

It cost us about £1 to get in, a lot in their money, then when we got inside we found we were in the most amazing club I have ever walked into in my life. There were oval wooden bars dotted around all over a large room with optics and drinks being served from in the middle of each one. More to the point, on every bar there were lasses stood dancing in high heels pants and bra. 'Are you happy I made you come in here now Mr Smith?' I asked him.

It was difficult to work out quite what was going on, especially as we were very drunk, but it seemed like a 'normal' nightclub and not a strip joint or anything, and these seemed to be the normal punters who were dancing on the bar in their lingerie. Was this a Russian thing? I was not sure, but I was not complaining. There seemed to be lasses just in the club and they kept their clothes on if not on the bar having a dance. As it turned out, we had stumbled upon the famous Hungry Duck club.

> 'Moscow's Hungry Duck bar was for a few brief years in the late 1990s the planet's craziest and most infamous bar. The only bar known to have been denounced in a national parliament (over 30 times) and subject to countless police raids, witness to hundreds of brawls and more bare-breasted women than a Hugh Hefner house party, there has never been another bar quite like it anywhere. It boasts among its accolades such titles as "only bar ever denounced in a national parliament" and single-handedly defined new limits of debauchery as young Russians threw off the shackles of the USSR together with most of their clothes.'
>
> Article from roadjunky.com

How unfortunate, or fortunate for us, that we were among the last visitors, as it was subsequently to be closed by the Russian parliament in December 1999.

The Duck did not disappoint. It was a regular nightclub but just full of people going crazy and really enjoying themselves. The Russian girls all wanted to be with foreign guys (how awful) as they expected them to have money to splash around. I think we stayed in there for about five days. Well for quite a few hours anyway before heading back to the hotel after a long day.

Wednesday seemed to be the day of the lock-in, and all will become clearer. We compared notes on the events of the previous night, where it seemed that me and Smithy had made the right decision to bail out. Boycey, leaving the bar, had grabbed a bin in the street and thrown it at a shop window. Luckily for him it did not go through but instead it bounced back. He would probably still be in the salt mines now if it had broken the window and the Russian authorities had got hold of him.

Anyway, after the breakfast stories and tucking into the moose, the Russian lads were meeting us for a few beers at lunchtime before we went our separate ways for the game. We headed in to Moscow, met them at the underground, and they took us for a few beers in a few backstreet bars. After two or three beers we settled on a funny little bar with metal curtains at the rear entrance. When you went to the toilet it was funny little place like a TARDIS, with a little door in to it, but when inside it opened into a larger room with a sit-down toilet that was up on a raised platform with three steps up to it. I think there was also a sink and urinal in there.

We were all just stood around talking and drinking in there, and had been in there an hour or so, then I suddenly realised that Roy was missing. Nobody had seen him for a while. He must have gone for a dump, someone said. It was bizarre because I remembered that the bolt on the toilet had seemed a bit dodgy when I had gone for a leak. I went to the toilet door and sure enough Roy was in there but not using the toilet – he was stuck in the bog.

'Thank God, I heard you ask where I was, I have been stuck in in here about 15 minutes. The bolt has snapped or jammed I can't get out,' says Roy. 'Okay, hang on, I will go get the barman.' The barman comes along and then it is comedy gold.

Speaking in Pidgin English he says, 'On the door there is a bolt! Yes?'

'Yes,' says Roy.

I'm Roy - get me out of here.

'Pull it from the left to the right.'

'Don't you think I've tried the bloody bolt! Get me a screwdriver,' shouts Roy.

'It's no time to be drinking Roy, we need to get you out of here first,' I reply. I then go 'Roy, I think we have a way of getting you out.'

'Okay,' says Roy.

Then in my best Pidgin English-Russian accent I say,

'Roy, there is a bolt, pull it from the left to the right.'

'Fuck off you twat,' says Roy.

'Mr Roy, you're not like that when we go gooseberry picking together,' I say, laughing. 'Right Roy, the good news is that we can get you out. A big Russian lad is up for kicking it in. Bad news is the barman wants £50 for a new door.'

'Just get me out of here,' says Roy.

Meat could not wait to jump into action so he took a big stride and kicked the door clean off its hinges. Perhaps that could have felled a giant Kojak. Roy was really pleased to be out at last and we had another couple of beers. We had arranged to meet some of the others at the hotel, so we headed back before going to the game.

At the hotel we were in the bar having drinks, Mally went off to his room to get something. Over an hour and a half later he had still not returned. Despite looking no one could find him anywhere. Two hours after going, he returned to the bar. We all asked where he had been.

It turns out that as the hotel had two sets of lifts quite a way apart (one for odd-numbered floors and one for even-numbered floors) and he had gone to the wrong lift shaft, but a member of staff had said he could go in the service lift which stopped at every floor. She opened it up, set him off, and then he had got stuck in it. He said it stopped and he could not get it to start again. The doors would not open, there was no phone to ring for help and he was in there for nearly two hours until someone called the lift and he managed to get out. It turned out that because everything was written in Russian, he could not understand it and all he had needed to do was to push the button to open the doors. He returned home telling everyone how awful Russia was, his whole opinion of the country coloured by two hours in a lift. The rest of us were very sympathetic about his ordeal, as you can imagine.

It was time to be sorting out getting to the game. Taxis had been ordered and somehow as organiser I had drawn the short straw and was to go with Boycey in the last taxi to the ground. It seemed that one thing Russia always seemed to be was dark. As our taxi pulled up outside the ground it was very dark and there seemed to be thousands of lads dressed in black jackets everywhere. I said, 'Right Boycey, best behaviour required, no gobbing off,' and we set off through the crowds to find the Leeds end.

We got in without any problem and there were about 1,000 Leeds fans there, which was a very good effort given the work required to be invited into the country and to get a visa. Leeds won the game comfortably, 3-0, and for me it was memorable for the way Michael Bridges led the line as the lone striker which was to be a trait of the whole UEFA Cup run that year.

In the ground the only issue seemed to be at half-time where people were saying that we had to leave our area and go to a toilet block amongst the Lokomotiv fans. It seemed that a few people who had been across had been attacked. We said we would go across and we would make sure we guarded the entrance so went over with eight of us, and four went to

Roger's cheap round Moscow – Rouse, John Higgison, Roger Allison, Toby, Boycey and Roy.

the toilet whilst the other four guarded the entrance. We then swapped over and the Russian fans milling around did not bother us.

After the game we had a few beers in the pubs between the ground and the hotel with the Lokomotiv fans we had played football against.

Thursday was a definite split between the parties as one group wanted to do sight-seeing and another party wanted to do more pubs. We agreed to go our separate ways and meet at the bar in town during the late afternoon.

We had a walk and took in a few bars in the group I was with. We were then walking between bars when we found a newsagent stand that was selling bottled beer and one of the lads, Roger Allison I believe, managed to get his round of nine large bottles of the local lager for about the equivalent of 60p. We drank them in the street with temperatures around freezing point.

As we drank our beers news of the draw for the next round of the UEFA Cup started coming through and it was unbelievable news; we would be heading back to Moscow in a fortnight to play 'Spartak, wink, wink, wink'. No one could quite believe this.

A few more beers were consumed before we headed to the bar in town that we had been in. We were well on our way and the drink was flowing.

One particularly memorable moment was Toby wearing a Russian hat. He had put the flaps up on the hat so they looked like rabbit ears and he was hopping around with both feet together, sticking his arse out and wiggling his bum like he had a bunny tail.

I think Toby and Boycey had then been in the back room on the dancefloor. When they came back to join us, Toby was laughing. He proceeded to tell us that a bloke with a moustache had come up and kissed Boycey. He said it was not a little peck, and that the bloke had proper kissed him on the lips and Boycey let him. We all started winding Boycey up that he had enjoyed it and we were not sure if they had those sorts of bars for him in Moscow.

Boycey was drunk and he was getting madder and madder as we teased him. He began waving his pint pot (one of the old pint glasses with a handle) about, saying that he would wrap the glass around the fella's head if we wanted him to. We told him to calm down and that we were only joking, but you could tell he was on the edge.

Next thing, the bloke who had kissed Boycey appeared. He had a moustache like Saddam Hussein and a smile like Felix the Cat. He wanted a few more pieces of Boycey, and was either very drunk or blind. This caused a commotion as we tried to keep them apart. Boycey clearly had feelings for him too, but it was clear that his feelings involved wanting to hit the Russian with his pint pot. Before the fella could take advantage of Boycey, the barman got involved and the local was evicted from the premises.

As the aftermath from the incident was settling down there was a class take on it from Chrissie who declared that Toby and Boycey had led him on. Firstly, Toby was doing a sexy rabbit impression and wiggling his bottom provocatively, and secondly, they had danced together for quite a while, so it was little wonder the poor man was confused about their sexuality.

Just as it had all calmed down, especially the laughter from Chrissie's verdict, the door to the bar opened and the bloke had come back in. Boycey was stood with his back to him at a high table and he walked straight up and grabbed his balls from behind. Thankfully, I got to him before Boycey could with his pint pot and I pushed him back out of the bar into the street. It was a very narrow street and soon he was backed up against the building opposite. It seemed half the pub had followed me outside.

As I let go of him, he prodded me in the chest and declared, 'You are one sexy motherfucker!' Toby was right behind me and was saying, 'Chin him!'

I said, 'I can't hit him, I'm too busy laughing.'

I think I just told him to do one, and he was basically very drunk but at least he was honest. He was ushered away again by the barman and we returned inside. I am not sure about Boycey, but Felix still writes to me every year. We had a couple of beers and a laugh about it in the bar and then we moved on.

The next memorable event was in a downstairs cellar bar when according to some we were a little bit boisterous. What we did not realise was that three of our party had tickets for the ballet. They said whilst they were there before the show had commenced, they could hear a commotion and could tell it was us making a racket by the voices coming from below. Hopefully, the music drowned us out or we had left and did not ruin the ballet performance.

We met some of the Lokomotiv lads for a final beer as we were heading home the following day. They were as bemused as us that Leeds would be returning in a fortnight.

I was still joking with the keeper about his save and we said our goodbyes and headed back to the hotel.

The return journey was uneventful, and we could look back on a truly memorable trip, one of my best European experiences with Leeds.

Prague, 2000

Everyone was looking forward to the quarter-final tie with Slavia Prague, as at the time Prague was one of the prime destinations for stag parties due to the prices and night life. It was not to disappoint for the visiting Leeds fans as we managed to get there before it became more commercialised following the Czech Republic joining the EU. It is still a top destination and many Leeds fans have made return visits, I went for my 40th in 2003 and other subsequent autumn trips when Leeds were not playing in Europe.

Leeds had beaten Slavia Prague 3-0 in the home leg on Thursday, 16 March 2000.

We stayed in a hostel in the heart of town, not far from Wenceslas Square. The first day and night before the game we simply went on a monumental pub crawl, sampling the cheap prices and pubs and bars of Prague. The cheapest drink we got was 37p for a pint in a back-street bar. It was a relatively incident-free evening by our standards; the lull before the storm.

The real fun and games kicked in on matchday. Firstly, in the hostel, we were in a room at the end of a corridor. We were utilising shared bathroom facilities but ours were a long way down the corridor, whilst the ladies' toilet was next door. In the night a few of us had popped to the loo while no one was around. However, Toby decided to go into the ladies' the following morning, as nobody was in there, and whilst he was in the cubicle three girls went in there and proceeded to use the communal showers. He said he had to stay in the cubicle until they were completely showered and left. It was awful for him, as his view was a little obscured and he had to wait in there for at least another 15 minutes for the next two ladies to arrive for their shower! His version was that he had to stop in the cubicle and wait until the coast was clear and had not looked. The red mark on one side of his face, where it was pressed against the door, we said was a clear giveaway.

After Toby had cooled off a little, we had another pub crawl pre-match from the lunchtime until it was time to head up to the game. Slavia were borrowing Spartak Prague's ground for the game so there were two sets of local fans milling around. Toby and Boycey had broken off to continue drinking with a group of Leeds fans whilst myself and Sage headed into the game.

Leeds, being 3-0 up from the first leg, seemed to be coasting but made substitutions and from looking comfortable ended up 2-1 behind. As we had quite a few beers and the tie had already been won we decided to leave early. I broke one of my usual rules, which was not to drink in the nearest pub to the ground. Sage and I headed to the pub down the hill nearest to the ground. There was quite a few Leeds supporters drinking in the bar as well as a few locals. About 15 minutes after we had arrived, Toby and Boycey landed with a group of about 20-plus Leeds fans they had been boozing with in some other pubs in the area around the ground. They

Old Town Square – Paul (Tommo) Thompson, Sage, Toby, Rouse, Smithy, Boycey.

Toby, Rouse, Smithy, Boycey, Keith Major (Sage).

mentioned an incident where a Prague fan was wearing a half-and-half Prague and Manchester United scarf, and he had received a slap to advise him of the errors of his ways.

This is when the fun really started. Some Leeds fans were at the front of the pub smoking and someone shouted, 'Hey lads, look at this.' I went out to have a look and there was a big, tall bloke walking straight down the middle of the road. He had a knife in one hand and something else that looked like a gun in his other. A Leeds fan ran at him up the road and threw a bin at him. I thought that if it was a gun, it wouldn't have helped much. Before he got to the bottom of the road two police cars raced to the scene, the police jumped out with their guns drawn, and after being made to get on the floor the bloke was arrested and taken away.

More Leeds fans were outside the pub now, and a few locals were milling about on the other side of the road. There was a bit of bemusement all around about the incident but no real sign of any more trouble. Five minutes later, though, about six van-loads of riot police pulled up and got out. They made a semi-circle and started walking towards the pub. I decided that making an exit may be a good idea but as I was leaving up the path a lad in front of me, who was doing the same, was hit with a police baton on the back of his head. There was to be no easy escape route. All the Leeds fans tried to get back into the pub and there was a real crush at the doorway. I backed away from the police as I was not turning my back and getting a baton on the head.

The crush to get in cleared just as I was getting to the door and I was about the last one back inside before the door was slammed shut. Not for long, though, as the riot police kicked it in and burst inside. As they did there was a hail of pint glasses and the sound of smashing glass and bits of glass flying everywhere. Quite a few were smashing off the riot helmets of the coppers. The first one in to the pub was nearest to me and was reaching out trying to grab me. I backed away all the way until I was at the rear wall in the front bar. He continued to follow me all the way and grabbed me and led me outside. They did this to everyone in turn until they had emptied the pub. One lad, who had a broken arm, had been sat on the toilet, but they kicked the cubicle door in and grabbed him from in there.

Outside we were all made to stand with our arms up above our head against the wall for what seemed an eternity. It's far harder than you would think. If your elbows dipped down even for a second, then it usually meant you would get an elbow pushed sharply into the back of the head to make you put them back up. There were a few strange things going on; Toby had been hit with a baton and was in an ambulance at the scene being looked at by a paramedic. Boycey was wandering around behind the coppers saying, 'Why haven't you got me?' Stan Julien, from police intelligence unit, was in the line-up against the wall trying to tell them he was a copper. Eventually he managed to show them his warrant card.

After a while Stan informed us that they just wanted us out of the area for our own safety; they were not arresting or deporting us. In the end they brought some police buses and put us into two groups. The group me and Sage were in was dropped at the Hilton hotel where the official Leeds fans were stopping. The second group were booked in to a police station then dropped at a tube station on the edge of town. Toby

Old Town Square.

informed me that when he had a DBA check for his work, this appeared on his record, so they must have recorded something about the folk in his van at the police station. After being dropped off me and Sage had a couple of beers in the Hilton and then headed to The Old Town Square and the central bars.

Rouse and Tommo.

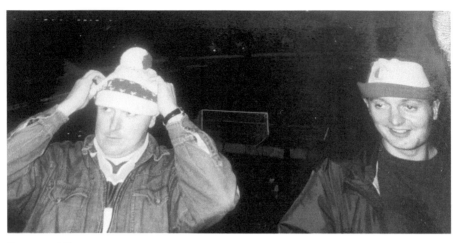

Rouse and Sage.

When we got to the square our party regrouped as people turned up over about a half-hour period. Toby now had an air-conditioned polo shirt that was ripped from the armpit to his waist and was covered in blood stains following his tangle with the police. There were quite a lot of Leeds fans drinking in the bars around the square. I had a nice pint, which I said to Chrissie, who had joined us, that I was hoping to relax and enjoy.

Next thing, two groups of local men and women decided to have a fight between themselves. For whatever reason, a few Leeds fans decided they needed to get involved including Boycey, who always had to poke his nose into other people's business. They decided to give the lads fighting a slap irrespective of what side they were on. Then it got surreal and funny. A female in the group of locals had lost her rag and she was going up to people and attempting to scratch their faces with her nails. She approached Boycey and without hesitation he punched her with a fast, straight-arm punch to the face and she went down like a sack of spuds.

A few of the locals were having a go at the Leeds lads and a very tall, gangly fan knocked one of them out. He then threw a hook at the next one who ducked, and his punch continued round and cracked Boycey who was stood a little too close. The local lad who was with the woman Boycey had decked ran up with a chair and stood facing the big Leeds fan with it. I was thinking, 'You'd better use it and then run.' It was crazy. He just stood there threatening to use it but did absolutely nothing. The Leeds fan reached over and took the chair off him, and then threw a massive uppercut that lifted the lad clean off his feet. He basically ended up sparked out just next to where me and Chrissie were sat. I said, 'Oh shit! Looks like we're moving again before police arrive.' I quickly finished my pint and said to the lads that we had best get out quick.

We wandered into the back streets and found a bar to get out of the way. It turned out that the punch had caused a decent cut above Boycey's eye on his eyebrow. I was feeling very under-dressed with no blood stains or wounds while walking about with Toby and Boycey. The big Leeds fan and his mates had also found the bar we were in and he saw Boycey's cut and laughed, 'Oh, sorry Boycey did I do that to you.' He was a larger-than-life character with the deepest comedy villain voice you had ever heard. We had a few pints in the back-street bars, then we ended up in a strip club.

When we were entering the club some Leeds fans were leaving saying that there had been an issue in there. There had been a scrap between some fans and the bouncers, involving the use of pepper spray and baseball bats. It all seemed quiet now and the staff were quite relaxed, so we went in. Even Toby was allowed in sporting his new designer-fashion ripped t-shirt.

It was a good club with a few bars and down one end was an area where there were lots of pretty girls dressed in basques. They were sat on some stair-like ledges. It appeared that you took your pick of the ladies, paid your money at the bar and were then taken into a back room. After we had got a beer, we stood near a table with a couple of other Leeds fans. Toby started talking to a woman near the entrance to the back rooms. She was dressed in jeans and a baggy t-shirt, and her physique may not have quite suited the basques worn by the girls on the ledges.

Toby disappeared into the backroom with the woman. Boycey, the whole time he was gone, kept saying, 'Can you imagine what he is doing now? The dirty bastard!' He repeated this a few times. One of the lads

Smithy, Roy, Sage and Rouse.

Rouse, Toby and Smithy.

Rouse, Rachel, Smithy and Will.

stood with us said, 'I was going to be good until you started going on about it but bollocks to it!' and he went to pick a girl from the shelf and disappeared into the back rooms.

When Toby reappeared from the back room, it turned out Boycey was wrong about what he had been doing. He had clearly found the

Will, photobomb, Smithy, Rouse and Rachel.

designated first aider. Toby says, 'I paid my money for half an hour but because of the cut on my head and the blood on my shirt she spent most of the time washing my hair, putting a plaster on my cut, and washing the blood off me.' I guess he owed £30 for the time he had spent in the shower at the digs.

After Toby's expensive clean-up, we had a few more beers in the bars on the way back to the hostel. We bumped into some other Leeds fans from Harrogate including 'Porno' Roy Flynn. The lads with him were enlightening us to Roy's pony girl fetish. They said they had been in a lot of clubs with strippers performing but Roy seemed completely unmoved by it all. Then in one bar a girl had got a whip out and wanted a volunteer to whip her bum. Roy was straight out of his seat and at the front of the queue. Apparently, it was the whip and ponytails that did it. I did not even know a 'pony girl' fetish was a thing until then!

The next day was more beer before heading to the airport for the flight home. It had been another eventful trip and cemented Prague as a destination of choice for future trips.

Leeds had also won a UEFA cup quarter-final and were now to be in the semi-finals.

Sage and Tommo have both sadly now passed away. Rest in peace, both great lads and part of the Leeds family. Marching on together, forever.

9

Galatasaray, 2000

This is one of the hardest parts to write about and part of me wanted to just miss this game out, but it is part of the journey that as Leeds fans we went on and we will never forget the tragic events that unfolded on 5 April 2000. The incident not only impacted on football fans but everybody who knew someone who may have been there. I lost count of the messages and contacts from friends and work checking that I was okay when I looked at my phone the morning after the tragic incident.

Christopher Loftus and Kevin Speight will always be remembered and never forgotten by Leeds United and all fans.

This chapter, in line with the rest of my book, simply recounts my memories and experiences of that trip. I was in Istanbul but not directly involved in the incident so I cannot begin to imagine what it was like for some of those lads who were.

Although it was a UEFA Cup semi-final, the demand for this game did not seem as high. I'm not sure if it was the previous reputation of Galatasaray for opposing supporters or the fact that the games had come so thick and fast that the use of holidays and the expense was taking its toll on people's ability to travel. Indeed, I had already used some holidays from this new leave year to get the Prague trip in.

The travelling party on our little gang was me, Stella, Dave Baron, Jonathan Walker and Corrinne Dixon. We went with Unofficial Football Tours again, arriving on Tuesday lunchtime, the day before the game.

I knew it would be a flying visit of one night out, matchday and then back the following day. I had an aunt who was living and working in

Istanbul, but I did not arrange to see her as I did not think there would be time. She had worked at the Craiglands Hotel in Ilkley, a place where Don Revie had taken the great Leeds team ahead of home games for many years. She had then moved on to work in the hotel trade all over the world.

The most memorable part of the journey there was that it was the worst flight I had been on for turbulence. At one point the plane had to drop about 10,000 feet in next to no time, to get out of the path of some bad turbulence. I did not think much about it at the time, but a lad sat next to me said, 'Nothing those Turks can do to us can be as bad as this!' After returning from the trip, I reflected that he was wrong.

On the bus to Istanbul there were some little cards being handed out with instructions for people to all head into town and meet up in Taksim Square. Stella, always one for a quiet drink, said we would not be going there then, and we would head for the old town.

Once we had booked in to the hotel we headed out to the old town. We had a good pub crawl and some food. The only incident we had was Dave Baron trying to buy a magic carpet from one of the local market traders who came up to our table outside a bar to try and sell us his goods. He was persistent and very reluctant to take no for an answer. I seem to remember Dave having to do a quick walk around a carpet display in a shop. I am not sure if the bloke bought us a drink to try and seal a deal. What the hell he thought we would do with a roll of carpet on a pub crawl, God only knows.

The old town was an area that it seems was mainly frequented by supporters of Fenerbahçe, another of Istanbul's football teams, so the locals were all friendly and wishing us well for the game against Galatasaray. We had quite a few drinks and visited a restaurant and it was a very good night out. As it got towards midnight though the old town seemed to be shutting down and it was getting harder to find any bars that were open.

As we were looking for another bar, we bumped into a Leeds fan getting out of a taxi. He had been up at Taksim Square and had returned to get some more money from his hotel. 'You should come up there,' he said. 'It's buzzing; far livelier than around here. It is like a proper modern city with neon lights like Piccadilly Circus, not sleepy like it is around here.'

We waited for him to get his money and then we jumped in the taxi with him back to Taksim Square. When we got out he said, 'I don't know where they all are, it was busy full of Leeds when I left.' He was right. It was very modern compared to the old town but it seemed very quiet. I'm not sure what had happened but when I turned around Stella was sat in the back of a minibus. There was a copper stood at the front door. It had sliding windows that were open, so I said to Stella, 'What are you doing on there?'

Stella says, 'The copper said to get in for our own safety and the bus will take us back to the hotel.'

I went to speak to the copper and said, 'Does he have to go back to the hotel?'

He said, 'For your safety we will take you back to the hotel but no you don't have to go.'

I said, 'Right, we've not had any trouble, we are fine thanks.'

I went back to Stella, 'Right, get off, he says you only have to go back if you want to go back.'

As we were still talking in the square, Wilko and Nige, two lads from Thirsk who travelled on our bus came out of the Pizza Hut. Same as the other lad they said, 'Where has everyone gone, it was full of Leeds when we went for something to eat.'

Everyone was a little bemused by the sudden absence of Leeds fans. We decided to go for a drink and headed for a bar. The bar had quite a lot of locals in and whilst we had our pint you could sense that we were about as welcome as a fart in an astronaut suit. There was just a strange atmosphere we had not encountered all night from both the bar staff and the people in the bar. We moved on and as we went around the corner of the street, we came across an entrance to what looked like a club. I walked in first and the entrance took you on to a platform area at the top of a metal stairway down into what was a huge room. The bar was at the opposite side of the room. Looking down though it was rammed with hundreds of blokes and not a female in sight. I said, 'Lads, I don't know about you, but I am not right up for drinking with this lot.'

Everyone agreed that it did not look like a good move and we decided to get taxis back to the hotel to drink there. When we arrived back, we headed for drinks in the bar. I am not particularly proud of the next set of events but in my defence, I was completely unaware of the circumstances of the night at the time.

One of the lads running the trip came into the bar and he was in a real state. He was going around telling everyone that two of our lads had been stabbed and we were going to fly out and not go to the game. He did not really say how bad it was and I guess I was imagining some of the 'less serious' stabbing incidents encountered by some of the Leeds fans in Rome.

He must have been in shock if he had been at the scene but when he came up to us at our table saying we were going to go home the following morning. I said, 'Look you soft Manc git, we are off to the game, we are not leaving! We are here now we must go to the game.'

Once it became clear the next day what had happened, I totally regretted what I had said to him. I never got the chance to speak to him in Istanbul, but I did apologise to the lad when I saw him in Madrid the following season.

When the full tragic events became clearer, the next day was one of the strangest I have ever encountered following football. There was total uncertainty as to whether the game would be played and if we would be allowed to attend or would we just be sent home. The Leeds fans meant to come out on the day of the game had all their flights suspended so only those already in Istanbul would be there, if any did attend at all. The one thing that was clear was that we were to be confined to barracks and we were not being allowed to leave the hotel.

We had breakfast and then decided we would test the lockdown. Two police with machine guns were outside the front of the hotel. We went through the kitchen area and attempted to get out of the building via the fire exit, where we were met by more armed police. We had no option but to stay in the hotel for the duration.

So the four of us ended up sat at a table in the hotel drinking wine, which was about all that they had to sell us. We got through a ridiculous amount between four people and had a genuinely nice steak meal at some point in the day to break up the drinking.

Eventually it became clear that they were going to play the game and that we were going to be able attend. If we would be able to see it now after all the wine was a completely different question. We must have been on the wine from 11 o'clock in the morning to six o'clock in the evening. Not great preparation for watching a match.

Buses came to transfer us from the hotel direct to the stadium. When we arrived at the ground it again all seemed very surreal even for a set of drunks. As we got off the buses there was a line of tanks and soldiers forming a barricade around the street and in front of the entrances for the away fans.

We were guided towards and then poured in to the away end through the turnstiles. Somewhere there was TV footage shown on the news of Leeds fans arriving and I think you could just about make out me holding Stella up and trying to get him through the turnstile like one of the blokes getting a horse in to the starting gates at the races.

Inside the ground the Leeds fans turned our backs on the game, something which is now recognised as a mark of respect for Chris and Kev. It was a surreal atmosphere to play in so God knows what it was like for the players. The game seemed to pass very quickly and as we know we ended up on the end of a 2-0 defeat.

At the end there was another military operation to get us not only away from the ground but out of Turkey. It was bizarre and was something I had never seen before. We were taken on the buses straight on to the runway, we bypassed all security checks and were put straight on to the planes and flown out of the country in double quick time.

We landed at Manchester to drop a few off on the way back and then took off and landed at Leeds. Again, flying from Manchester to Leeds was something I had never done. I am not a wine drinker and all the travelling, taking off and landing was taking its toll. The take-off from Manchester was the final straw and I was in the toilet being sick before we managed to get too far away.

RIP Christopher Loftus and Kevin Speight. You never expect to go to a football match and not come back home again.

* * *

I lived with my grandparents for quite a while and my aunt was the youngest daughter. We were quite close as I was growing up. My aunt, who had moved on to work for Intercontinental Hotels all over the world, had met and married a Turk in the 1970s, much to my grandad's displeasure. As a result, we had holidayed in Istanbul and visited Marmaris in 1979.

Her husband's father was a major in the Turkish army. Turkey back then was a country of haves and have nots. His father had a massive house on the edge of Istanbul with security fences and barbed wire around it. There were people outside the complex living in tents and herding goats. They told me at 16, if they get in, they will rob and kills us.

My uncle was so disparaging about his own people and the class system was clear to all to see. The lower class were seen as worthless lawless peasants.

It was clear in 2000 that not a lot had changed, the very modern buildings and money was evident in Istanbul but as soon as you drove into the streets away from the centre it was run-down ghettos with poverty clear to see.

Anyway, that is just context to what happened later that year, when my aunt still lived in Istanbul. At Christmas 2000, the whole family in the UK was at my uncle's in Harrogate and he said, 'Your Aunt Kate is on the phone, she wants a word.'

I went on the phone and she said, 'You came to Istanbul and you did not visit us.'

I said, 'It was literally a short stop-over. We were there for the game and straight back; there was not really time.'

'One of our friends is the Galatasaray club doctor,' she said.

'Well, what do you want me to say?' I asked.

'Our lot sorted your lot out,' she said.

'Sorry! What did you just say?' I asked.

'Our lot sorted you lot out,' she repeated.

'Our lot? Are you trying to be funny? Fuck off!' I said angrily and passed the phone back to my uncle.

I have never spoken to her again since that call to clarify what the hell she meant by that statement.

10

Munich, 2000

Following the tragic and disappointing end to the 1999/2000 season, Leeds had qualified for the Champions League but we had to play in a qualifying round. Typically, we did not get any easy draws and were up against 1860 Munich from Germany.

On a personal level, my second daughter Jasmine was born on 26 July 2000, so Mrs Rowson had a newly born baby and a toddler (Samantha) aged 18 months running around at home to look after whilst I went off to enjoy myself. Plans were put in place for her mum to go to York and stay with her whilst I was on my three-day European trip.

This trip was also like the time that Don Revie put out what everyone thought of as the traditional great Leeds team line-up of Sprake, Reaney, Cooper, Bremner, Charlton, Hunter, Lorimer, Clarke, Jones, Giles, Gray sub Madeley against Mansfield in 1970 – it was the only time that 11 actually played together.

Well, this was the one and only time that myself, Charley and Toby ever went to an away European game together. What could possibly go wrong? I should have known!

It started in a strange way as well. On the Monday night I was crown green bowling for Black Swan at Pateley Bridge and after the game we had a few beers in the Royal Oak pub just up from the green. Whilst in there the whole Nidd valley was plunged into darkness by a power cut. It was very romantic drinking by candlelight as the valley was in darkness for a good hour. After getting back to Harrogate, I met Charley for a pint in the Black Swan and then Toby was picking us up at closing time to drive us to Stansted where we had an early-morning flight to Munich.

Toby was gagging for a drink and playing catch-up so after a pint or two in the bar at the airport he hit the miniature bottles of red wine on the plane.

We got to Munich and headed to find our hotel, which was not too far from the train station. We booked in and I think it was about 2pm when we headed out for a few beers. There was a boxing-themed bar straight opposite, so we headed in there. We spoke to a couple of Leeds fans and a British guy living in Munich. There had been talk of a large Turkish population in Munich and he said to watch ourselves on a night as a few gangs of them would be around the town.

We moved on and after another pint in a bar which was in a mainly shopping area, we found ourselves in an outdoor market where we had a stein of lager and some food. A lively group of Leeds fans came into the market and sat down quite near us. Once they had headed off, we thought we had best head for a quiet drink (Stella-style) elsewhere to try and avoid any potential trouble, or rather make sure we could get into the bars.

About ten minutes after the group had moved on, we left, and on the way we asked a local the best bar to go in. They recommended the Hofbrauhaus, so we went in that direction. I had a habit of buying baseball caps of the opposing team we were playing for Mrs Rowson (she could not say I never brought her anything back but also the hats were useful for getting in places at times) so I popped in a shop and got an 1860 Munich baseball cap. Meanwhile, Charley was laughing his head off as usual as he had seen a postcard rack which had cards of Concorde. In July, Concorde had crashed with over 100 Germans on board while leaving Paris. He could not believe they were selling these cards and he left us to go buy one. We said we would see him in the pub. Famous last words.

Toby and I found the Hofbrauhaus and sat outside near the street so we could look out for Charley. However, when Toby ordered three steins the waiter put them down inside on a table right next to the lively group of Leeds fans who we had seen in the market earlier. Toby came to tell me to come inside as he could not carry them. Moose, originally from Harrogate, was sat at the table with the lads. We had a chat with him, and he was saying that they had been in this bar the night before and had some hassle with the bouncers. Most were hungover and quite subdued, but three of the lads were carrying on at the front of the bar; they were pissed, high or both. They started doing Basil Fawlty's German walk up and down the length of the bar. There was a little bit of singing from the other lads but that was about it. It was not long before someone said they had rung the cops. It seemed that within no time at all the German police swooped and there were lots of them as they entered the bar. The three lads doing Basil Fawlty impressions had apparently realised the bar staff were ringing the police and had got out before they arrived. That did not bother the cops as they proceeded to try and round everyone up who was a Leeds fan in there.

As I had my 1860 baseball cap on and there was a large indoor beer garden behind us, I started to walk away into the background. I think I would have got away with it too if it had it not been for 'my mate' Toby who shouted, 'Rouse, don't go that way, quick, over here, the fire exit is open.' The cops had seen me now and realised I was with these other lads, so I ran with Toby and we went out the fire exit. Of course, it was straight into the police who were waiting outside it!

We were rounded up by the police and taken to a minibus that they had parked outside. They asked us where we were staying, then they took me and Toby back to the hotel. They wanted us to collect our passports. They came with us to the room and made sure that was all we brought with us; we had to leave our bags. I left my 1860 Munich hat in my bag when I got the passport. I did not want them to think I was wearing it to get behind enemy lines. That cap was later to confuse Charley when he returned to the room.

It was then on to the police station, and all 13 of us were booked in. First, they made us take a breathalyser machine test. It was funny as virtually everyone recorded seven, eight or nine on the scale until Toby blew into it and recorded somewhere around 27!

'Bloody hell, Toby, what have you been drinking? You drove us to the airport, is your blood pure wine?' I asked him.

'I just had a few bottles of wine on the plane,' he said.

They put us in a large cell together for the night. I think they put a couple of trays of horrible stale bread in the cell at one point. I remember only one of the lads liked it and was asking for everyone else's. We were guessing as they made us get our passports that they would deport us.

However, the next morning we were proven wrong. First, we were all taken one at a time to be assessed by a doctor and then to see a woman who had the job of drawing everyone's tattoos. She said of the 13, I was the only one without a tattoo to draw. As a result, I got a cup of coffee and a chat as it would normally take her ten minutes and she

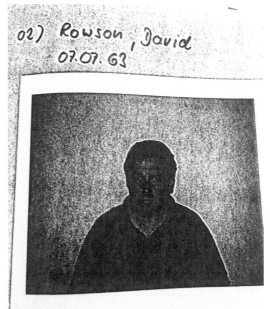

knew I would not want to go straight back to the cell.

A bit later that morning they decided they would interview us all as well. I was the first one to be quizzed. There were two coppers, plus me and a German translator. It became apparent this was all about an allegation of us making Nazi salutes which is against the law in Germany.

Rouse arrest picture.

117

Summary sentence

The public prosecution charges you of the following state of facts:

You belong to the english hooligans-scene. On 22.08.2000 about 17.00 o´clock (5.00 p.m.) you were in Munich in Hofbräuhaus am Platzl.

2

You stayed in a group of about 30 english hooligans, by which songs were sung and slogans were bawled out. Over a period of 30 minutes persons of this group, amongst others, you too, by raising the outstretched right arm showed the so-called Nazi salute and called the slogans „Heil Hitler" (Saviour Hitler) and „Sieg Heil" (Victory Salvation). You participated here by showing several times the Nazi salute and by shouting repeatedly „Sieg Heil".

You knew that these were gestures and slogans of the national-socialist tyranny and that they must not be used publically in Germany.

You are therefore accused of

having publically used marks of a national-socialist organisation,

Charges.

I explained to them that Toby, Charley and myself had travelled separately to the match and were not with the group. It was just coincidental that we were in the same pub and we had been waiting for our friend. I also said that the group of lads had done nothing and that the few fans who had been messing about and who the bar had rung about had already left when the police arrived.

They had taken a camera off one of the lads in the group and proceeded to place photographs in front of me on the desk. I had to try not to laugh out loud as the lads had taken a team picture outside their hotel; they had all got German army helmets on and were all doing a Nazi salute. It was clearly in jest but what could you say. I simply said, 'You see, I am not on the picture, we travelled here separately, as I have said.'

They then asked how well I knew Moose. I was assuming this was as they had him down as a name amongst the Leeds lads. So I explained that I had run a Leeds supporters' club branch, and when younger he used to come on my bus to the games. We are originally from the same town and I occasionally see him, but I do not go to matches with him anymore.

After my interview I was taken back to the cell and Toby was next up. Shame I did not get to speak to him first, as when we compared notes after he had made me look like a complete liar. In answer to how well he knew Moose, he had said, 'I have known him for years since he was this high, he is one of my best mates.'

'What did you say that for?' I asked. 'Because he is,' says Toby. 'Didn't you wonder why they were asking you about Moose?' I asked him. 'No, but he is my mate, it was just the truth!'"He's my mate too but I was not going to tell them that! They were asking for a reason,' I said.

We still were not sure what their plan was to deal with us. We soon found out when around teatime on the Tuesday of the game we were informed that we were all to be taken in turn in front of a local magistrate. The lads were all guessing if the order was significant. It soon became evident that it did not make any difference, as basically we were all being told we were off straight to prison, we would not receive £200 and we would not pass go. We were to spend one more night as a group of 13 in the police station and then Wednesday morning we were loaded into a prison van and all transferred to Stadelheim, Munich's main remand prison. We had all been given a piece of paper that basically said we could be kept without trial for up to three months but could have a verbal appeal before a judge once every seven days.

We were put into the booking-in process at the prison and at one point, as we were in a waiting room, there were about 20-plus large blokes in bright orange overalls who all looked like bodybuilders in the next room.

'I think we are in for a kicking,' said one of the lads. The kicking did not materialise, and we think they were just prison staff being nosy and seeing who this group being checked in were. We came out of the room and went into a medical assessment process then were issued with our glamorous prison outfits – a nice blue cloth ensemble.

As we left one of the rooms we were split up and it would be the last time we were all together for a while. I was sent up through the prison with one of the Doncaster lads and we were in another holding area. A stocky little Turkish guy was put in the room with us. 'Were you in Istanbul?' he asked. 'Yes, we were,' we both said. He seemed to be trying to wind us up, but we were not taking the bait and we closed out the conversation with him. We were from there taken on to our wings.

As I got to the wing the guard walked me along the corridor, and as we got near to the door of a cell there was a tall black guy (he must have been 6ft 5in) walking towards the cell. 'Not in there,' said the guard, 'you are being moved to a double cell, this guy is having your cell.' Great, I thought, in for Nazi salutes and I am pissing off a big black guy as soon as I arrive on the wing.

So my new home was a single cell with a window looking to the outside of the prison, over farmland with crops in it. It had a bed, a toilet and a sink.

Next to the bed, on the wall the former occupant had painted a bright sun shining over a tropical island scene with a calm blue ocean, sandy beach and a beach hut bar. Above it was the words 'Man Mountain Etna', so I assumed that was him. He had pictures of Pamela Anderson serving at the bar in his beach hut and she was also laid in various poses on his beach.

We had all been scattered across the four wings and floors of the prison. I was on the wing by myself at first. It was a 23-hour lock-up with just one hour for exercise a day in the yard at the centre of the prison.

On the first morning, the Thursday, we all got a visit from the British Consul. For me this involved me being taken back through the prison system and put first into a holding cell to wait. As I walked in to the cell there were nine Turks sat in there and just one seat on the end near the locked door was for me. The little stocky Turk who was coming in to the prison at the same time as me was sat on the opposite bench, a few people down the row.

He decided to speak to me, 'What do you think of Istanbul?'

'What do I think of Istanbul? I went on a holiday there when I was 15 in 1979 and it was a shithole! I went again this year and it is still a shithole!' I said.

Another Turkish guy intervened and said to me, 'Right calm down, just ignore him.'

Shortly after the exchange of words I was taken in to see the British Consul representative. He was going to allocate each person a solicitor to try and help with getting us out. He asked how the hell I had managed to end up inside prison in Germany when I had two young kids at home. I asked him to ring Val and get her mum to stay on to help her. It was the only moment it proper hit me what was happening – the fact that I was meant to be home around that time. I had been dealing with it quite well and matter-of-fact. There was not a lot I could do about the situation, it was all out of my control and I just needed to take each day as it came, go with the flow and to try and get through it the best I could.

When the British Consul rang Mrs R the conversation went along the lines of:

'Hello, this is the British Consul in Munich, your husband is being held in prison in Munich. We do not have a date for his release yet so cannot say when he will return.'

'Oh, you are very funny!' she said laughing, 'Who is this?'

'This is the British Consul in Munich, Mrs Rowson, and this is no laughing matter. This is deadly serious.'

When they had rung Val, her dad was there picking her mum up to take her back to Harrogate. I was due home that day, so she was literally putting her bag in the car to go. Val had to shout her to get her not to go. She then had to take her bag back out and stay for a little bit longer. Val was breastfeeding the new baby and had a toddler so could not even get out to shop. Her mum unpacked and settled back in again.

Following the meeting with the British Consul, I was taken back to the wing and then almost immediately it was time for exercise in the yard.

When we went to the yard the guard who had taken me to the wing pointed out a young lad who was English. His predicament made me feel that I had it easy compared to him.

He had finished university and one of his mates from London had got them a free holiday, courtesy of his uncle, to go to the West Indies. All they had to do was bring some sensitive machinery in cases back home for him. Of course, they were stopped in Germany and the cases were instead full of drugs. He was facing up to a possible 15 years in prison, he had been told by his lawyer.

Aido and Rouse in Leeds in 2019.

That day I also got a new wing man, Aido, who was one of the three doing the Basil Fawlty impression in the pub. They had got away but then when they turned up at the ground for the game they were arrested. They had been identified because of the pictures on the camera and had now been fast-tracked to join the rest of us in prison.

Aido became the life and soul of our wing and I must admit he helped me get through the stint in prison just through laughing at him. He rarely shut up and was either shouting out of his cell window across the prison to the other Leeds lads or announcing the arrival of the food deliveries with his usual 'McDonald's, we have Big Mac, nuggets, chicken burger, milkshake, come and get it.'

The guards seemed as bemused as us that we were in prison and had not just been deported. They were saying that they would send us home soon as nobody went to prison for this offence.

You could send letters out of the prison, but they had to be in capitals with no joined up writing and they all had to be reviewed and checked by the

Letters home.

Dear Val, Samantha & Jasmine

JUST WRITING TO LET YOU KNOW I AM
OK AND HOPE TO SEE YOU ALL SOON.

WE WERE HELD AT A POLICE STATION FOR
TWO NIGHTS AND THEN MOVED TO MUNICH
PRISON ON THURSDAY.

I HAVE PLEADED NOT GUILTY OF THE OFFENCE
BUT AS I WRITE THIS FRIDAY LUNCHTIME
I DO NOT KNOW WHEN THEY WILL HOLD
THE TRIAL.

TOBY IS ALSO HERE ALONG WITH 11 OTHERS
ARRESTED AT THE SAME TIME. I AM IN A
CELL ON MY OWN HOWEVER, AND THERE ARE
VERY FEW ENGLISH SPEAKING PEOPLE.

THE BRITISH CONSUL SAW ME YESTERDAY
BEFORE I WAS TAKEN TO THE CELL. THEY
HAVE ARRANGED FOR A LAWYER TO COME
PERHAPS TODAY.

I AM HOPING THE TRIAL WILL BE MONDAY AND
THEN HOPEFULLY I WILL BE RELEASED BUT
AT THE MOMENT I JUST DON'T KNOW.

I HOPE YOU ARE COPING OK AND THAT YOU CAN
GET PEOPLE TO HELP YOU OUT WHILE I AM
AWAY FROM HOME.

First letter home.

German authorities. I sent a couple to Val but also used them to put forward my account of what had happened, as a subliminal statement or evidence. The letters also gave me something to do, as life got tedious very quickly.

I had a second meeting with the British Consul where he said Val wanted to know what to say to work. I said to just get her to say we had a family issue as they would probably think the baby was ill and I needed to take some time off. Luckily, it was a double bank holiday across the Monday and Tuesday, so I missed less time than I would have. The British Consul told me they had appointed a solicitor and he would visit me to discuss the case.

Toby told me afterwards that following the call from the British Consul his daughter had rung his work and said, 'My dad's in prison in Germany and we have no idea when he will be coming home!' She was honest.

The weekend came and there was still no sign of getting out. We all agreed to ask to go to prayers as they had that option for all prisoners once a week. We were going to meet up in church on the Sunday but then because we had all requested it, they cancelled it for all of us. They obviously thought we were planning a jail break from the church.

The solicitor came and spoke to me and went away saying he would be back with a plan of action.

Aido told me afterwards about his experience checking in to the prison. He was with another lad and they were put in a holding cell overnight with a German prisoner. They had abused the German all night and the next morning he was cowering in the corner of the cell when the guard came in. The guard asked what they had done to him. They said they had done nothing. The guard said, 'You would not have done it if you knew what he is in here for.' They asked what he was in for and the guard said, 'He murdered his wife with a shovel.' 'Well thank fuck that he did not have a shovel,' they said, laughing.

As the days passed, we had started to make friends with a few on the wing. The lad from Dover on remand for drug smuggling was in a cell with an Austrian called Oliver (Olly). He had lived in Germany and run an accountancy firm with some German guys. They had all been charged with tax fraud or evasion, but the Germans were on bail and able to set up and run other businesses. He was still held on remand. He had been for two years and he could have been for another 12 months as the case was complex and was not ready to go to court. He said it was how Germany treated foreign nationals. Of the 3,000-plus in the prison, only about 300 were Germans. Bloody hell, and we were in for being Nazi racists. Hitler was Austrian so maybe Olly was being punished now for this too.

Olly had a top cell with a TV and everything. Aido was trying to negotiate with the guards for a move for me and him into Olly's cell as one guy had left prison and they had two spare places. If he could not wangle that he was telling the guard that me and him would like to be in a double cell. I was stood behind him shaking my head at the guard. As much as I liked Aido I liked the peace of my own cell and could hear him and laugh at him entertaining everyone from a distance. I was not sure I would feel the same about it if this had been happening constantly from within my own cell.

Olly seemed to have some influence with the guards, and he had even managed to get me and Aido a pass to go over to their cell for a meal. Being invited for dinner in prison is very rare, Aido informed me. We never got to go though as we were released before it happened.

Aido and me had done our **Max and Paddy** shower trip out together. There was no Raymond the Bastard or other prisoner-related incident. A shower was a luxury allowed once a week otherwise you were just to wash in the sink in the cell.

Mind you, we were not as close some cell-mates. Apparently two in the party were avoiding drinking too much of the water as it contained bromide to hinder your performance and they were regularly comparing notes to check the impact on their little friends. Cute, Toby, we will keep your secret. Well maybe not. It amused the lads in the football team we played in no end that it took Toby about seven days for him to start to turn by comparing his willy with his cell-mate's whilst locked up in prison.

When we got out, I found out that I had apparently been tipped by some of our party as the person least likely to cope with prison life. I'm not sure what their criteria had been for reaching this conclusion, but we had a lad threatening suicide saying he could not cope after about two days and Toby on the turn.

Some of the lads were on a wing with German neo-Nazi skinheads. We had made the German newspapers and television news, so they clearly thought we were Nazis. The lads put them straight and left them clear by their response that we were not.

We had been arrested on Tuesday, 22 August, had been in the remand prison from the 24th, and by the 31st we were still not sure when we would be going home or be taken to court.

I had got out of the habit of reading books but during cell time I was reading the ones that you could pick up off the daily trolley round on the wing, and listening to Aido shouting out of his cell window. The food was generally awful, including raw fish as one offering which went straight down the toilet. There was only rice pudding and chocolate pudding that were anything to look forward to, a bit like school dinners back in the day.

I wrote some letters to Val that I kept and took home as I was sure they would take too long to get there in the post. I did suggest that next time we could all go away as a family, so I clearly had no intention of not going on the Leeds trips again. The consul had visited on the Tuesday and passed back a message from Val. It felt great to receive contact from outside the prison.

There were two twins from Donny inside with us and they were released on 31 August as they could not be identified because they were identical, even though they were dressed completely differently. There were rumours that we may get released with a large fine, but no one was sure.

Just as we thought we were going to be in for yet another week we were all summoned to the office and we were thrown out with charge

Hoping to be home soon to give you all hugs and kisses

Dave.

x x x x x
x x x x
x x x
x x
x

P.S. Next time to europe you will all have to come along!

P.P.S. I assume you will have contacted or been contacted by Charley. It will be interesting to hear what he had to say about Munich

P.P.P.S 16.55.
Just got back from seeing the consul, your message re work gave me re assurance that there is life outside this prison.
Still confusion over when — it would appear the two twins have gone — news to the consul she was still talking about Friday to me. Told her to tell you I would do the shopping Saturday!

End of second letter.

sheets issued to us. Fines reached 4,000 euros including a bill of 150 euros for the pleasure of our nice prison hotel stay.

We had ended up in the police station and prison for 11 nights, so I think I lost about a stone and half. At one point I had to change my uniform size as it was falling off me. It was a good pre-season routine for Sunday morning football. Toby and I were player-managers for our

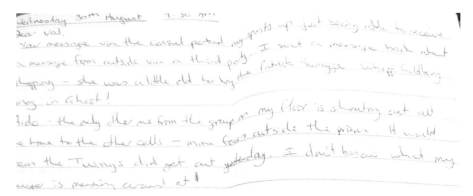

Extract third letter.

Sunday team first and second teams. In the first week of the new season they only managed to get one team out with us missing and had to cancel the second team game.

We had to go to the British Consul to get a flight back arranged and then a hotel for the night.

We were not sure if it had made the news in England, if the police would be waiting for us when we landed in the UK and if there would be any further action taken against us. I was thinking that my job could be at risk. I did think I would have to write the story and sell it to the press, or really go after the Germans for wrongful arrest in the worse-case scenario.

A lot of the lads would not go out the night we were released, so they could not get into any more trouble, but me and Toby had not had a night out in Munich, so we hit the town big-time that night and ended up in a club until the very early hours.

The next day at the airport, one of the lads had news from home that he had a big pay-out on an insurance policy and he suddenly hit the beer. We got on the flight back to Heathrow and the lad who had been drinking heavily since his good news took a dislike to an American passenger in front of him. He threw a punch at the bloke, and thankfully it missed. We could have been put down in Paris and had another stint in a foreign prison.

We got to Heathrow and Toby had agreed to give the lad and another kid a lift back home but that involved getting from Heathrow to his car at Stansted. I said I was off to King's Cross as getting the train straight to York will be quicker.

I got the tube and a train from King's Cross. I was home. I had left on Monday, 21 August and arrived back on Saturday, 2 September. Mrs R's mum was stood down from support. I needed to take Monday and Tuesday off work to just get my head around what had happened and being free again.

In all my European trips I had not encountered anything quite like it. It was not quite over either as I had the small matter of a €4,000 fine and a solicitor's bill to deal with. Not to mention wondering what would happen if work needed me to visit Germany at some point in the future.

Someone had rung Val and she told them we were being detained in Germany. It was a bowler and word spread that I would not be playing in a bowls competition on the August Bank Holiday as part of the Starbeck

Unused match ticket from 1860 Munich v Leeds United.

gala day in Harrogate. A lady at my work had found out via a bowler friend and bumping into me outside as I was leaving one day a couple of weeks later, she said, 'Do not worry. Your secret is safe with me.'

At least I had an unused match ticket, which are valuable collector's items I understand.

Back to Charley, who had gone to buy his postcard of Concorde to send home, although he did not end up buying one. Maybe he thought it was in bad taste, especially in Germany. Mind you, this is the man who turned up on a ferry to Hamburg in a jumper bought for him at Christmas by his family with RAF planes all over the front. He said he had not even thought about where he was going when he put it on. Anyway, minus the post card he set off to find the Hofbrauhaus.

As he got close to the bar it was clear something was happening as there were riot police everywhere. He went down another street with Big John from Kippax and went to a beer garden. There was also a reporter from Calendar, John Shires, with a TV crew down there. They went in to the Hofbrauhaus for a drink and saw some other lads from Harrogate, but no one had seen me and Toby. He had a few more beers with the Kippax group and then ended up in a park with a bar and can remember nothing until the following morning (par for the course).

He saw my 1860 Munich baseball cap and thought we had been back to the room and then gone out again. He had asked if we had been back and reception said yes but not that we had been accompanied by the police.

He went into the bar opposite the hotel and the barman said, 'You were on form last night.' Charley does not remember being in the bar on the night. He bumped into Stella and Phil Buchan in a pub and Lai joined up with them later. It was not until he got to the match on the Tuesday night that people told him there were rumours of 13 fans being arrested and deported. He thought we had just stayed out partying all night.

When he got back after the game the local Turks were making a noise in the street below the hotel, keeping him awake, so Charley decided to

Charley and Stella find out Rouse is in prison.

drop his empty beer bottles on them from a great height in the dark to clear them off.

Charley went on a trip on the Thursday to Dakar concentration camp with Alan Watson and Tony Bune. We had not booked a hotel for the final night as we were flying back quite early so Charley had to check out and put all three bags in left luggage. He asked Alan and Tony if he could crash with them or if they would take the bags. It was a resounding no! They had a strict landlady, they said. It did not go unnoticed and was commented upon when I next saw them.

Charley slept in the airport but almost overslept and had to join the end of the queue for the flight. As he got to the front the flight was declared full. They ripped up his ticket and said he was being upgraded to business class. He was tucking in to a full English and sampling the free wine while Alan and Tony had standard-class offerings and we were trying out the prison food out.

Charley enjoying Munich.

Alan and Tony took our bags back on the train while Charley headed into London and got the National Express back. The bags were returned at Boro away, and Porno Roy got them back to York, which was something I only found out writing this book.

I should have known though as it seems he likes to pop around for a coffee. I was working at home one day and after a knock on the door I found Porno Roy on the step. 'Oh, what are you doing here?' says Roy.

'I live here, Roy! What are you doing here?'

'Thought you'd be at work. I was passing and just thought I'd pop in for a coffee with Val.'

'Well, you best come in then. Shall I make myself scarce,' I joked (I think, given the content of the letters home; an elephant never forgets).

Tony Bune and Charley.

11

Milan, 2000

For this game I had an early departure as I had somewhere to visit for a Monday-morning appointment on the way to Milan. I left home on the Saturday morning to head to the Liverpool game at Elland Road. I was living in York and there were reports of epic floods in the city. Rather than go straight on the ring road to Leeds, I heard on the radio that the floods were at their highest point and that Clifton Bridge may have to be closed to traffic. So of course I went for a look. There were police by the bridge and sandbags lining the banks. It was quiet and nobody stopped me from driving across. It was an impressive sight; as I looked left and right the water was at my eye level at the top of the sandbags. The view seemed just like looking across a flat sea in both directions over the river valley with the banks seeming a long way apart.

I had to stop at traffic lights on the far end of the bridge and that was the only time I felt worried. You could see the water was millimetres from the top of the sandbags. If the water had come over the top, I reckon there was a good chance I could have ended up in the sea past Hull. It really was an impressive appreciate-the-force-of-nature moment.

The next impressive force-of-nature moment was seen at Elland Road that lunchtime in the guise of Mark Viduka, who scored four goals to beat Liverpool 4-3 in what was a great game of football.

Straight afterwards, I was heading to Stansted to catch a flight to Munich. I was returning for a trial on the Monday morning to attempt to clear my name of the charges imposed on me from the 1860 Munich game.

I drove the car to London, parked it up, and I was then getting an overnight bus to get me to Stansted for my flight on the Sunday morning. I do not know what it was in those days about the selection of airports. It always seemed travelling miles to get the cheapest flight was the right choice. Perhaps back then there was a far bigger difference in flight costs from Leeds Bradford, or less choice.

I had felt the need to try and clear my name as I had a €4,000 fine hanging over me but also in case work ever required me to go to Germany for any reason. Most of the lads who were with me in the prison in Germany had just ignored the bill they were given.

I had been liaising with my allocated solicitor in Germany and was also armed with a written letter from Stan Julien of West Yorkshire Police, saying I was not a naughty boy and not known to them. Part of the evidence from Munich had stated that he had come to the police station and identified us all as top category C football hooligans. Stan advised me that was not the case, as whilst he had visited the police station when we were all arrested, he had made no such statement. Stan had told me that West Yorkshire Police had advised him not to get involved but he said I would be entitled to sue him as an individual officer if he had provided a false statement. He had become well known to the family, and Mrs R said, 'Oh, he's such a nice man when he rings up.' Clearly he was living up to his Hot Chocolate reputation from Bolton when he was wearing his silver suit and the Leeds end was singing 'You Sexy Thing' to him.

My work had not been aware of what was happening with the trial. I had taken leave to cover my absence. There was a daft incident where one of my colleagues joked about me being very well known to the police due to me going to games. Around the time that I had to pick my letter up from Stan at Holbeck police station, I was going to a works event at South Leeds Sports Stadium. As we were sat in traffic at Dewsbury Road a car in front clipped a woman's car and sped off. She chased it and both cars turned down towards the stadium. We were following behind. Both the cars drove past the entrance. I said, 'She will catch them, it's a dead end up there. We had best check she's okay.'

The car had spun around and was facing her car and a youth had jumped out and was swearing and shouting at her. As he saw our car pull up he jumped back in his. My colleague, who was driving, had opened his door and was just about to get out. 'Shut your door!' I said. 'Why?' he asked. He found out as the car swerved around the woman's car and screeched off back down the road. It would have taken him and his door with it. We checked the woman was okay and my colleague gave her his number, then later in the morning we got a call and had to go to Holbeck police station to provide our details if required. While we were in there Stan came in and said hello to me. My colleague joked that he knew I was a football hooligan and known to the police. 'I have just seen him at away games, they know everyone,' I replied.

Anyway, back to the trip. I took in the London late-night life, having a few pints near Victoria station, and then got the overnight bus to Stansted for an early-morning flight. I got to Munich late in the morning and went and booked in to my hotel. On the Sunday afternoon I had a good look around Munich and visited lots of the places I had missed out on seeing in August. In the evening I decided to visit the Hofbrauhaus and do a little bit of research for myself. I spoke to a couple of bar staff who had worked the day we were arrested. Both said there was not a lot going on and they thought the reaction of the staff and the police was well over the top. They could not believe we had been jailed as a result. I had a good look at the layout of the place.

After I had concluded my Jim Rockford private detective act, I could relax and have a few steins, something again I had missed out on in August. Unfortunately, as it was a Leeds away trip, I got drawn into partying too hard with a group of Brits in there and overindulged. On the Monday morning I woke up in a mad panic having overslept and I nearly missed my own trial.

I did get there just on time. As I entered the building, I could hear shouting and the judge was having a right go at my solicitor. He was saying that this was a waste of public money, and that no football hooligan was going to travel back to Munich for a trial. My solicitor was saying that I was coming. 'He rang me yesterday and he is in Munich already.' It was never in doubt, well except for the partying on the Sunday night!

Anyway, the trial could now start as the main exhibit was indeed in the building. The prosecution had similar problems as two bouncers from the pub were witnesses and only one of them had turned up. Conveniently for the 16 arrested, eight had been identified by one bouncer and eight by the other.

The judge asked me some basic questions to identify me and then got the bouncer on to the witness stand. Luckily for me it was the bouncer who had identified me on the day of the incident.

'Is this one of the football hooligans you identified?' asked the judge.

'Yes,' he replied.

'Does he look the same in appearance as he did on the day of the incident?'

'No, he had a skinhead haircut.'

The judge sent over to him and the prosecutor a copy of my file containing the pictures taken from the police station. They had taken photographs of all of us. I have never had a skinhead cut in my life, never mind a few months before. It was virtually as simple as that. My solicitor said his piece and showed them the testimony from Stan Julien, his colleague and also one from Stella as secretary of the Harrogate branch.

The judge adjourned the case, spoke with the solicitor and I then returned to the solicitor's offices with him to discuss next steps. He basically said he expected the charges to be dropped and the judge was offering a 'no case to answer' verdict. This was important in German law as it basically gave them protection against a wrongful arrest case. The solicitor said to get a full clearance and a wrongful arrest case against them

Dear Mr. Rowson,

enclosed you find the main part of the files of the enquiry.
As you can see Mr. Vollath (back of page 25) and Mr. Imhoff
(page 30) say that you have shown with your hand again and again
the „Hitler-Gruß".

The prosecutor Mr. Von Hunoltstein also says, that Mr. Stan
Julien and Mr. Darren England had told him, you would belong to
the fan-category C.

What do you say to that?

Can you contact Mr. Julien and Mr. England and ask them, if that
is true? Should they say, it is not true, they should give a
written statement to you and you should send this statement to
me.

Concerning to the videos I intend to watch them occasionally.

The trial will be on 6th November 2000 at 9.15 a.m.

Please send a written statement to me. Subsequently would you
please call me (best time is in the afternoon). Then we can
decide if it is necessary to see you one more time before the
trial.

Letter inviting me to trial and an extract from trial pack.

Staatsanwaltschaft
München I   23.08.2000

Pol.Az: 8553-001831-00/6

Vermerk

Heute habe ich die szenekundigen Beamten / Fanbeamten vom Leeds
United (Stan Julien und Darren England) befragt, ob sie Erkennt-
nisse zu den 13 festgenommenen Personen haben. Die Fanbeamten
machten zu den einzelnen Personen folgende Angaben:

WESTOBY, Stephen: Fan der Kategorie C — LAWYER

ROWSON, David: Fan der Kategorie C

TAYLOR, Myles:

Fan der Kategorie C; gegen ihn besteht für ganz England ein Ver-
bot Fußballspiele zu besuchen; in England ist gegen ihn ein grö-
ßeres Verfahren wegen KV und Schwarzhandel mit Eintrittskarten
anhängig.

Trial pack cctv images.

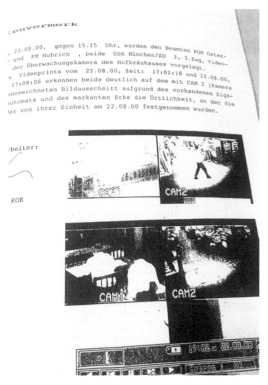

would require me to return to Munich and it would involve a court case lasting five days. He advised me against it, saying they would not want to lose the case, although he said they would do everything they possibly could not to lose and would look to get me on a technicality. He said if I was staying in Munich for the trial that they may even attempt to set up an incident involving me whilst I was in town to makes sure I lost.

It was quite staggering for a solicitor to be so open in his views of the public authorities in Germany. However, with Leeds still in the Champions League and a lot on at work, I could not afford the time for any long court cases. If a consequence of the arrest had been to lose my employment, I probably would have felt very differently about pursuing it. Stan had said that the files of all of us arrested were sent to the Home Office as they had requested them after the incident.

The solicitor said we should keep pressing for evidence until we got the verdict through formally in writing. ITN had some footage from inside the pub that one or two people had seen on the news. Some people had seen a clip of myself and Toby leaving the building walking with the police. They did not know we had been arrested as we were not handcuffed or being held by the police. ITN wanted £750 to provide a copy of their footage from the scene, so the solicitor was instructing the prosecution to provide it and pay for it.

I thanked the solicitor and then proceeded to have a very good Monday night out in Munich too, partying in a few bars.

On the Tuesday at 9am I got the train from Munich to Milan, arriving about 4pm. The journey took a fantastic scenic route through the Alps. The views are stunning.

Even though I was travelling alone, Rouse Tours had still booked a travelling party in to Milan. I was in a night earlier than the rest of the party who were arriving on the Wednesday.

When I got to Milan, I headed to find the hotel. Stella and Smuff were already in Milan having made their own way there. Smuff had agreed to leave his mobile phone on so I could find them on the Tuesday night when I arrived. After checking in I headed out and found a phone box as I did not have a mobile in those days. I tried Smuff twice but just got his answerphone.

I left a message saying, 'Well done Smuff!! I am not going to be able to find you now in Milan am I you idiot!' We had not exchanged details of where each other were staying so I thought that was that, and I would not see them.

I had a bit of a walk from the hotel and saw quite a few bars. I was ready for something to eat so I decided to go back to an Irish bar I had passed. I walked in and as I approached the bar, I had to do a double take. Three people were sat drinking at the bar: Stella, Smuff and a friend of Smuff's. I stood next to them, ordered a pint, and when they looked round hearing my voice I just said, 'All right, guys.' Smuff and Stella did not bat an eyelid, 'Now then, have you been in Milan long?' 'No,' I replied. 'How did you find us?' That is a very good question. 'Of all the bars in all the world you walk in to this one.'

We had a pub crawl, and it turned out Smuff and Stella were staying at the other end of town so it was total luck they ended up drinking near my hotel. I'm not sure how many bars were in Milan and what the odds of that happening would have been.

Officially the police were closing all bars in Milan on matchday. We had a good night including some whiskey cocktails and we made plans for getting into the bars with a few of the owners.

The rest of the Rouse Tours party arrived on the Wednesday morning so we checked out the bars we had lined up. We drank in our local district to make sure we could get plenty of drinks in ahead of the game.

We had reached an arrangement with a bar that we would come in for food and beer. The first round was therefore 17 lagers and 17 pizzas. We then also ordered 17 carafes of red wine. We stayed in the bar as we were not sure how many other places would be serving.

The game of course was 1-1 with Dom Matteo's goal and 10,000 Leeds fans in the San Siro.

It was the night of players singing in front of the fans after the game. As Peter Ridsdale and the directors were departing, I could recognise a few people from the council. Ridsdale was chair of Education Leeds at the time and a few thought he had designs on becoming the first elected mayor in Leeds. He was at the height of his popularity before the financial crash and our fortunes imploding around him. He was certainly milking it and lapping it up that night.

We returned to our district to gain entry to another bar we had lined up and celebrate progressing to the second group stage. This one was an American bar and it stayed open until 2am. It did get rumbled by the police and I understand a fine was issued but the money we spent that night more than covered the fine.

We also revisited a little bar late on that was serving the whiskey cocktails and I am convinced the last couple of hours in there on the whiskey is what finished me off drink-wise after a heavy Saturday to Thursday stint on the beer.

The day after the game, we had to go to the British Consul as Max had lost his passport and needed replacement ID. This took quite a while and when he got home his passport was in his shoe all the time.

We got a train to Genoa as the party had flown into Milan but were going back from Girona airport. It was a terrible train journey. I felt so rough. I had run my race as far as drinking was concerned, and I think I was now alcohol-poisoned nearly to Eindhoven levels. We checked in to the hotel and whilst everyone else went out, I spent the night and next day in bed trying to sleep it off before heading to the airport and home.

* * *

I got a written response saying that I had no case to answer so the fine and charges were dropped. I paid the solicitor's fees except the cost for assisting the release from prison. I wrote to them and I said everyone got released by the courts and they had done nothing to earn

Letter confirming the charges were dropped.

GB-Yorck Y030 SPT

München, 00-11-10
Le/Ri

Our Ref: Rowson David

Dear Mr. Rowson,

I talked once more with the judge and the prosecutor. Both persons now will close the matter without any payment of your side. Merely you will get no compensation for the arrest.

There will be no further trial.

In my opinion the final order to close the matter will be issued during the next two weeks.

Final order to close the matter means that you are not sentenced and not punished in any way and you will not be registered.

Yours sincerely

that money, plus they had never revisited me in the prison as they said they would.

I put it all down to experience and just got on with travelling Europe watching Leeds, as you do. Whilst it was not pleasant and not something you would choose to do it is something that you can joke about after and I just had to deal with it at the time. Wrong bar at the wrong time and all that.

I did take exception to one of my mates who said, 'Well it was just a matter of time. The way things had been going it was inevitable!'

'How do you work that out? We were just sat in a bar having a pint, it could have happened to anyone.'

I assume he meant we had been experiencing some close shaves with Prague etc but it is water under the bridge now. I am, in the words of Billy Joel, an innocent man.

12

Anderlecht, 2001

On this trip were Toby, Boycey, Toby's lad Andy, and one of his mates. I'm not sure how it happened but Rouse Tours were stood down initially from any involvement in arrangements and Boycey was permitted to take charge of booking the flights. As there was no league game that weekend Boycey got us an earlier flight out on the Sunday. There was just one slight flaw in his itinerary as he had us flying back home on the Wednesday about 6pm.

As we were going through it in the local headquarters, the Muckles in Harrogate, I said, 'You have done well Boycey, good flight times, reasonable price. Just one problem.'

'What's that,' he asked.

'The game is 7.45pm Wednesday night so we'll be flying back during the game.'

We were basing ourselves in Amsterdam and travelling over to Brussels on the train. We had to quickly get another return flight but the only cheap one left was back in to Liverpool and we agreed that we would hire a car to drive back from there on the Thursday. The youngsters who were travelling with us decided they would stick to the original return flights, clearly more bothered about their trip to Amsterdam than the game.

When we arrived in Amsterdam, we had no accommodation, as Boycey's planning did not extend to this either. We walked down the main street from the station and somehow Boycey latched on to some bloke on the street offering accommodation who looked like a druggie. A scruffy git with a beard and a bandage across his face where it looked like he had recently been slashed with a knife.

He led us to a hostel-type place where we ended up with a room for five: three single beds and a bunk bed. The door to the room though was pretty much no more than a piece of cardboard, and was the thinnest wood you had ever seen. A firm nudge and you would be into the room.

So we then basically had three days on the beer in Amsterdam to lead-up to the game. This mainly involved Boycey annoying anyone he could during our time there.

Millwall fans were in the Hello Sailor Bar. 'Leeds and Millwall hate each other.' Okay, Boycey, these two guys are just here for a beer, they do not want to talk about football. He persisted going on about various games in the 80s where we had visited Millwall. He then proceeded to trip off his usual bizarre Millwall fetish. 'I would just like to go for a pub crawl around Millwall's area on the day of a match and ask them what they think about Leeds and why they hate us. Just have a pint and a few beers with them see what they are like.' Well good luck with that one, Boycey. Leeds fans fill you in when you are annoying so I am sure Millwall would be happy to oblige.

Next up he decided to try and entertain a Northern Irish bloke and his wife. 'What was it like living in the Troubles?' 'We are here for a break, we do not want to discuss it.' Again, it took a while to get him off the subject and away from them.

Boycey then had a good go at annoying himself, 'I am celibate. This is disgusting, all these blokes trawling the streets window shopping and going with the dirty bitches.' Okay, Boycey, you booked for Amsterdam, what did you expect? Herds of galloping wildebeest?

There were one or two highlights of the three-day stay. Toby, walking down the street, said something to a girl as we were walking past. She was wearing a long trench coat, turned opened it up, and gave us a flash of her outfit of bra pants and suspenders. I assume she was on her way to work and did not normally just wander around like that flashing at folk.

Rouse and Boycey.

Toby then took a shine to an Eskimo-looking lass who looked just like Bjork. He was singing to her in the street and then ended up with her following us around for a while. We worked out she was probably homeless and after money from him.

On one of the evenings, one of the young lads took a visitor back to the room, and after she had left so had Toby's son's wallet. This resulted in a visit to the police station the following morning and every receipt in Toby's wallet had to be brought in to play to recover his son's losses arising from that unfortunate event.

On the day of the game, it was quite late when we headed over to Brussels on the train and went to the city centre pubs for a few beers before the match. The young lads had stayed in Amsterdam and were getting the flight home. It was to be one our the most famous European nights with a 4-1 victory away from home.

Toby and Boycey

Toby leaving the Hello Sailor bar.

We got the train back to Amsterdam, and the evening there afterwards was to prove interesting. We needed to get the early flight so had been to the hotel and taken our bags out with us so we could finish the night out and get straight back to the airport.

Toby, Boycey and me were in the Hello Sailor Bar again sat around a table and Toby started telling us how his aunt had bought his son a car for £1,000. His son could not afford any insurance though and Toby was also sourcing him a fake tax disc. I was basically having a go, telling him he was stupid and if Toby knew that he was not insured he should sort it out or it could ruin his son's life if something happened that he would regret. Toby said he did not ask her to buy him the car, I said maybe not but to make sure he is legal. What if he has a major accident?

Boycey, sat at my side, decides he is not happy with what I am saying and says, 'What the fuck has it got to do with you? Shut the fuck up or I will wrap this around your head.' He is holding one of those old pint pots with the handle. 'If you are going to do it you best get on with it,' I say to him. It was a good job he did not sneeze as I was all for wiping him all over the pub, mate or not. Toby did his best to defuse the situation, but I was fuming and not a happy bunny.

As we walked across Amsterdam towards the station, I was just behind them thinking, 'Why do I come away with them? I have had enough.' They decided they wanted a kebab and we headed to a food place that was basically a window in a building near the canal. As they were ordering their food, I felt a sharp dig in my ribs. I looked around and there was a tall black guy stood behind me.

'I am Atlas, I am the nastiest man in Amsterdam, give me your bags and all your money.'

'Are you serious?' I asked him.

'Yes, I am the nastiest man in Amsterdam, and I have a knife,' he said.

It felt like his fingers to me in his pocket (not that I am an expert in fake finger weapons), but I decided to see what the brutal brothers made of it.

'Hey guys, Atlas here wants our bags and all our money. He is the nastiest man in Amsterdam.'

They turned around and the conversation went along the lines of, 'He is quite big but how long do you reckon it would take to tip him upside down in the canal?' 'I reckon 20 seconds.' 'No, he is big, I reckon it could be about 30 seconds.'

Atlas decided he had only been joking all along and started a conversation with us. It was classic Toby who then decided to offer him advice on mugging.

'Look, son, we are the wrong sort of people to be trying to mug. You need to steer clear of the likes of us. You'd be far better picking on little old ladies.'

My mood had improved. Nothing like a failed attempted mugging to cheer you up. This had been a very funny moment and reminded me why I did knock about with these silly bastards and enjoyed the trips so much. The threat of a pint pot around the head is nothing amongst friends.

Another trip over, well after the train flight and hire car to get home from Liverpool. We carried on living the dream!

13

Madrid, 2001

This trip was made up of people travelling at a variety of different departure times. Roy Flynn, Mally Appleyard, Nige Fawcett and Rachel had gone early on the Saturday morning. I left a little later having been to Leeds against Manchester United at Elland Road and then driven down to Luton straight after the match.

When I got to the airport, I found that my flight was delayed by about three hours. I met a lad from Barrow-in-Furness in the airport and we had a few beers at the bar. We were now not getting into central Madrid until about 11.30pm and he had not sorted anywhere to stay. I said, 'I think we have a quad room with three in so even if it is only for your first night you might be okay to stay with us.'

We got a taxi straight to the hotel. We found Roy and Mally in bed as they had been out already in the evening but had decided to return. We were going to head out on the town so after a little persuasion Roy got himself up and decided to come with us. You know it makes sense, Rodney.

As we were walking into the town, we were saying – well,

Mally Appleyard (Stan Bowles Calendar).

mainly my new friend was – that we would find a nightclub with music, a dancefloor, and ladies. Roy's face was a picture and I'm not sure that was on his itinerary, being the Pleasure Dodger of course. As we walked down through a shopping precinct our new friend said, 'Hang on, I can hear something,' and started scratching at some double doors. 'No, keep walking, there is nothing in there,' said Roy. Next minute the doors were prized open with his fingers and we were straight on to a nightclub dancefloor. We closed the doors behind us and went in. We got a few looks as we walked past people but nobody said anything and it looked like we were in for free.

It was a smart place with a Latin-American feel to it. We got a few beers in and then discovered our new mate was certainly a bit of a character. He wanted to chat up every woman who moved, which was fine, but not just the ones who were on their own – he decided they were all fair game even if the boyfriend was in close proximity. Roy said to me, 'Where the hell did you find him?' 'He's funny,' I said.

We did well to last about an hour and a half in there before he caused an international incident with some guy who took exception to him chatting up his girlfriend and we were asked to move on by the bouncer.

We had a few more drinks before Roy, on his second night out, had had enough and wanted to go back to the hotel. Barrow-in-Furness crashed at ours before he made his exit to go and find his accommodation. I never saw the Madrid nightclub specialist ever again. It was a memorable cameo though.

The Monday was mainly memorable for a lookalike dancer.

Roy phoning a friend.

In a bar in the middle of Madrid there was a flamenco dancing act where the bloke was the spitting image of Nigel Martyn. This was followed to a visit to a little back-street bar, where I was a little bit tipsy and one of the Leeds lads in there was the spitting image of a senior manager from work. I was about to go and check that it was not him when he disappeared into a back room with a young lady, so I thought I had best not disturb him. Finally, for the last drink we went to a bar where the staff were telling us that when Manchester United had played there their fans were arrogant pricks (we were not going to disagree) but that they said they had enjoyed having the Leeds fans in town.

On matchday as we had liked the bar staff's opinion of the red fans so much that we decided to head there for our first drink. At 10.30am! As we walked in the staff greeted us like lost friends having remembered us from the night before. I'd had enough of the lager so decided I would have a Bacardi and coke for starters. This was a fatal error. The barman said to tell him when to stop as he poured the Bacardi but someone from behind started to talk to me. I turned around and the tall glass was over three quarters full. He smiled at me and said, 'You never said stop!'

Now most normal people would refuse it, share it out or throw it away but no, silly bollocks just put the coke in the top and decided a good drink to start the day was a nearly neat half pint of Bacardi. We stayed in the bar for quite a while as they continued to serve good measures. Leeds fans were arriving all the time. We always seem to latch on to a song of the moment and 'play it to death', and the Madrid trip I will forever remember as the Johnny Woodgate Hokey Cokey trip. It seemed to be sung everywhere by everyone every five minutes. It was Kiko Casillia and Pablo Hernandez song of its day.

As we were in the pub, I noticed a familiar face at the other side of the bar. It was the Scum Airways lad who had been running the trip to Galatasaray back in 2000. He was stood with a couple of guys. I went up to have a chat with him and I basically apologised to him for my reaction the night of the incident in Istanbul when I had seen him in the hotel. I said I never realised just how bad it had been. He was fine about it, and he said he had probably still been in shock and thought he had been babbling and was quite incoherent anyway. We talked about the trips since and I said, 'Well Munich didn't go well,' and explained what had happened. One of the lads with him was an Everton fan and I said we had been to a few of their games as I played football with a lad in Harrogate who was a big Everton fan.

As it transpired, and unbeknown to me, this bloke was writing a book called **Scum Airways** about the Mancs running trips for Leeds fans to Europe and our conversation was now going to be in it. He basically twisted the conversation we were having and pitched it as a Leeds fan bragging about having been in prison in Munich and linked it to the undertones and atmosphere around travelling Leeds fans in Europe. When I was shown the entry in the book I was not best pleased and on one of my visits to Everton I was enquiring about him and would have been pleased to discuss it with him in person. At least Toby's dog had the same feelings about the book as when Charley leant him his copy the dog destroyed it.

We spent the day trialling the bars of Madrid but eventually the timing of starting drinking and my friend behind the bar's silly measures caught up with me. As the time to go to the game was approaching, I had fallen asleep with my head on a table outside a bar. People said they tried to wake me up, but I was out cold and so in the end they had to leave me. I must not have been out for long as I woke up, saw everyone had gone and decided I best try and get to the game. I tried to flag down a taxi but they were all busy. I was thinking this was going to be difficult as another cab flew past but then a car pulled up and a lad driving said, 'Are you going to the game?' I said yes and he gave me a lift right to the stadium. He was an Atletico Madrid fan and he wished us well.

We had bought tickets for the home end and I managed to get in bang on kick-off. It was a very impressive stadium and great to see the full Leeds end from the stand opposite. There were Leeds fans all over the ground and again an estimated 10,000 present. We put in a great performance but lost 3-2 including a handball by Raul and a freak bounce that beat Nigel Martyn.

After the game, I ended up getting off the tube in an area I did not recognise with a group of Leeds fans. We were drinking outside a bar but then the staff said we all had to go inside as it was illegal to drink outside after a certain time at night. I was drunk but it was a very surreal experience in the bar. There was a TV on and it flipped between showing pornography and random lively Spanish music. The bar staff had already said singing was not allowed or they would shut the bar, so the Leeds fans were humming the tunes of our songs but not singing. Then we took to mimicking the Spanish music that came on between the porn. There would be silence when watching the porn and as soon as the random Spanish music came on, they were joining in not singing but really loud la, la, la, la, la, la, la to the interlude music. As each interlude in the porn came the volume of the accompanying la, la, la, la, la getting louder and louder. It was very funny, and even the bar staff were laughing. In the end the bloke running the bar said, 'Oh for God's sake, sing!'

After leaving this bar I had a few more drinks on the way back to the centre. It was another lost-in-a-big-city moment though as I grappled with where to find the hotel. I was wandering around looking for a landmark when I was not paying too much attention looking behind me and managed to find some roadworks where the surrounds had been removed by some kind souls. I found myself in a hole in the ground. Luckily, I was not too badly damaged, and I was well anaesthetised from the Bacardi. I climbed out of the hole laughing at myself and limped back to the hotel to get some kip.

It was less embarrassing than as a young office worker being sent to the Post Office in town in the summer and walking straight into a lamp post whilst looking at a young lady on the opposite pavement. I think the whole street had seen that one based on their laughs.

So, the Bernabéu was ticked off the list of grounds and Leeds still marched on in the Champions League.

14

Valencia, 2001

So by this stage of the Champions League run I was feeling that I had taken out Spanish citizenship with yet another visit to the country for the semi-final against Valencia. As the trips were coming thick and fast and family holidays were being neglected a little bit, I decided to kill two birds with one stone and take Mrs R and the chilblains away for a week in Benidorm, which was just down the coast from Valencia.

But the trip did not get off to a good start! On the Saturday morning I was using the grill on the cooker, which was at about waist height, when my two-year-old daughter Samantha decided to pull something off the drier and a box started to fall towards her. Thinking it might contain something heavy that might do a young child some damage, I tried to move in two directions at once, to stop the fall of the box and put the grill pan down. Bang – and my back had gone badly. I was in agony and I was not even sure I would be able to drive the car at one point.

We flew from Teesside airport which at that point was pretty much just a field near Darlington. I'm not sure how I did not manage to buy any painkillers on the way to the airport but with two children, a double pushchair and cases, having a bad back did not make the trip enjoyable. The Spanish customs and coach drivers did not seem to be very helpful to say the least, they must have seen I was struggling but all turned a blind eye at my struggles, whilst Val had her hands full with the kids.

We got to Benidorm on Saturday teatime after a day full of me moaning and swearing in pain. We got checked in to the hotel and I was still in agony. I said to Mrs R that I was going out in search of drugs and if I could not find any then I would need to get pissed up to kill the pain. I could not find a pharmacy open, although I'm not sure how hard I looked, so I headed off to a bar. I had somehow avoided the Leeds v Arsenal result, so I found a bar to sit down and watch **Match of the Day**. My pain at seeing the Leeds line-up was nearly as great as the one in my back.

We had drawn 0-0 with Valencia in the first leg of the semi-final and we were second favourites to go through. It seemed Champions League football was a must, but we had rested players for a Premier League match, I assume to give us what they thought was the best chance of winning the Champions League. It was as if they were gambling everything on winning the competition to get back into it for the following season. I was fuming and could see what was coming as they lost 2-1 with an under-strength team out. A point would have done it at the end of the season and that was to be one of the worst decisions we had ever made. In my opinion it started our financial downfall and the downward spiral. The only good news was that the chef in the bar was a Leeds fan and when I told him about my bad back, he brought me a pack of Ibuprofen that he said I could have. That man was a hero! I had a few beers with him when he finished work and then decided I had best make my way back to the hotel.

Leeds fans were arriving in Benidorm all the time. I had arranged to meet up with Toby and Boycey who were travelling down on the train from Barcelona. One of the supporters who was in the prison with us in Munich (the one who threw a punch at the Yank on the plane) had opened a bar in Benidorm. I headed to meet them on the Monday with Mrs R and the kids. We found a pub packed with Leeds fans. The kids were fine and seemed to be enjoying it. Boycey was arseholed and started pointing his finger in the face of Samantha and then wagging his fist in her face as he does. Meanwhile the bar owner was doing rock a bye baby with Jasmine, who was only about ten months old. We had a few drinks with them and then left them to it.

Tuesday was matchday. I was getting the Spanish version of the National Express to Valencia and then planning on staying out and crashing over for the night. After breakfast I said, 'Right, I am off, I will be back some time tomorrow.' The coach took about hour and half, and when I had got off I jumped in a taxi and said, 'Take me to the area where the Leeds fans have been drinking.' The driver clearly did not understand that I meant the main square as he dropped me right outside the ground. I could not be bothered getting him to take me anywhere else, so I paid and went into a bar outside the ground.

I made another crazy drinking decision as I saw that they were doing steins of sangria. I'm not sure what attracted me – the steins (as in Munich) or the sangria (I had that loopy juice in Lloret de Mar 1984 on holiday with Chairman Charley). When I ordered they would not take any money off me at the bar, insisting that it would all go on a tab. A tab at a bar right next to the ground, what could possibly go wrong? After about four steins it was harder to get served so I left my tab open, was able to leave and went to the next bar just over the road. I found they were operating a tab too.

I met lots of Leeds from all over the place. At one point sat outside the bar we were doing the traditional screwing-up of a guy's interview by doing something stupid in the background. Then someone said, 'Hang on, what did you just say?' He informed us that UEFA had banned Lee Bowyer on the morning of the match due to an incident caught on camera in the first leg. This seemed like another kick in the teeth for our hopes.

As the day progressed, I basically had a free bar, constantly swapping between the two pubs and racking up my tab. As kick-off got nearer the pubs were rammed and there was no way of getting near the bar. I had to move on to an area further up the side of the ground, which was like a pedestrianised area. People were sat about and there was a bar with a hatch selling beer to folk outside. The guy selling was the famous Spanish drummer Manolo, seen on TV at Spain's games in the World Cup.

I was stood near the bar when a Leeds fan said, 'I think these six young lads are going to cause bother.' The group of Spanish lads had said to two younger Leeds fans that they were ultras and did not want people drinking in their square near their ground. I had a quiet word with them and said, 'Lads, I wouldn't bother if I was you. There may be a lot of older guys around with their wives sat around but if you have a go at any of the Leeds fans, I can assure you they will knock ten bells out of you. Just lighten up and enjoy the atmosphere, it's too nice a day for fighting.' They seemed to get the message.

I went inside the bar and Manolo was not going to serve me. 'You have been causing trouble,' he said. As it turned out, one of the Spanish lads I spoke to was in there and he said, 'No he was stopping any trouble.' So I got my beer in there and had a few drinks with the Spanish lad and his mates.

The match was turned by yet another Spanish handball but by the end Valencia were comfortable 3-0 winners.

Lai Lam and Manolo.

Crowd in Valencia Champions League semi-final.

After the game was over, we found a little bar near the ground. Our table was being shared with Harry Gration from **Look North**. He was telling us it was a definite handball and the goal should never have stood. The bar had closed its doors and at the front was a lad going bananas to get in. He looked like Wayne off **Auf Wiedersehen, Pet**. I had seen him around a few times. He was from North Wales. Harry Gration took an instant dislike to him, telling the staff not to let him in as he was very drunk. We then had a bit of a pub crawl on the way into the centre of town. If there is one thing we do well as Leeds fans it is to not let a bad result get in the way of having a party. By this time, though, my free bar for the afternoon was catching up with me and it all got a bit hazy. I was with Toby, Boycey and 'Harry', a train driver from Scarborough they had met on the train from Barcelona and travelled with.

I crashed down at Toby and Boycey's hotel; I think Boycey slept in a chair so I could have his bed. They reckon I was totally wasted, and I woke up handcuffed to the bed. They had to leave to get their early-morning train and apparently the lad from Scarborough always carried handcuffs. They had thought about leaving me handcuffed naked to the bed for the staff to find me. Thankfully, they thought better of it. 'Harry' probably wanted his handcuffs for a better victim.

I was sick as a dog before leaving the hotel and getting the coach back to Benidorm to resume the family holiday. I think I had it all on between Valencia and Benidorm not to be ill again.

Samantha showed me how it should be done on the way home on the bus from Benidorm to the airport. Mrs R had been buying some strawberry milk concoction for her to drink and she was sat on my lap when she let out a big burp and was then sick all over me. I had to travel for another 30 minutes before I could change my t-shirt and shorts.

So we were out of the Champions League, I was lucky to escape the clutches of the three perverts who had me chained to the bed, had a bad back on the way there and was thrown up over on the way back.

To be fair, the behaviour of the kids was not a lot different to that of the rest of the Leeds travelling support.

We finished our family holiday in Benidorm before returning home. I had not been joking when I said they should come on a trip.

15

Troyes, 2001

The trip to Troyes featured Dougie Kaye, Boycey, Toby and John (Everton Tommo) Thompson. It was a Ryanair special sold as a Glasgow to Paris flight, which was was really Prestwich (Stirling, 40 miles from Glasgow) to Beauvais (70 miles north of Paris). It met the criteria for the travelling party which was to go for three weeks and save a fiver. Toby and Boycey were always a bit pissed off if rooms were more than £10 a night.

We drove to Prestwich airport and then from Beauvais on arrival we travelled by train to Troyes. We tracked down a hotel as we had not booked in advance because every hotel could only offer double beds.

Stella and Dougie.

Dougie – don't call me Shirley.

We thought it would be different when we arrived but no, there were no single beds to be had anywhere. We quickly discovered that there were no hotels in town offering a room with single beds.

I must have drawn the short straw as I ended up sharing with Boycey and our double bed, whilst Dougie, Toby and Tommo were in another room with two double beds. We could only book for the first night, as it was a bank holiday in France and all the hotels were full on the night of the game.

Looking at the double bed when we entered the room, I took a pillow and a mattress and said, 'Right Boycey, whoever is back first gets the bed, the other one is sleeping on the floor.' I totally expected it to be me on the floor as Boycey can often get pissed up and peak too early. He always told us he was celibate, which figured as he looked like a cross between a monk, Gary McAllister and Nosferatu.

We headed off into Troyes and found some little bars to have a few beers in. We were walking down into the town centre when we bumped into Stan Julien, the police liaison, and a couple of other guys coming out of a restaurant. They warned us that there were gangs of Arab lads cruising for a bruising so to watch out for ourselves if wandering around, and not to get split up and on our own on a night. Boycey was perturbed that Stan had called him Andrew. 'How does he know my name?' 'Yes that is strange, as he has you filed under D,' says Dougie. 'D?' says Boycey. 'Yeh, in the file D for Dickheads.'

It turned out they were not wrong, as when we got a few hundred yards further into the centre there was a scuffle just kicking off and a gang of Arab lads running about. There were some Leeds fans in a bar opposite where the scuffle had taken place and we went in for a drink. There were about 12 lads from Doncaster in there and the crowd of Arabs over the road seemed to be growing all the time. 'We are glad you lot have arrived, looks like it might come on top,' one of them said. 'They look like mainly teenage kids to us,' we said, and got our beers in. The group had a young kid with them who seemed about 11 and was decked out all in Burberry clothing, including the baseball cap. As it got a bit more intense between the lads and the crowd of locals, he got a bit upset. Another group of ten older Leeds fans turned up and that was the signal for the locals to back off. They clearly did not fancy their chances when the numbers on each side were getting towards even.

We finished our second pint and decided to head out of the centre a little bit to find another bar. We next found a good place with music and a big Halloween party going on. This was to become base camp for the night as it was a great party atmosphere. As the party continued, we took a fancy for the Halloween decorations. Dougie got himself a fake hairy hand off the wall and I went for the whole skeleton outfit and mask look. We acquired these as we left for use on matchday.

Dougie, Toby and I were ready to go back to the hotel to our beds, while Boycey and Tommo wanted to stop out. We left them to it; maybe we thought the acquired goods may prevent us getting in the next bar.

I got into the double bed, making sure Boycey's bed was made on the floor. A pillow and a blanket bed were put all neatly in place and waiting for him to get back. I did not think anything more of it until I turned round in the middle of the night and there was Boycey's face large as life staring at me. A scary sight at best of times, never mind in a double bed with you!

I got up and went to the bog, and then I decided to sleep on the floor seeing that Boycey could not follow instructions and I was not going to sleep with him out of choice.

I fell asleep and I was woken up a few hours later by Boycey who was shouting, 'Wake up Toby you fat bastard.' I thought, 'He cannot even remember who he is sharing a room with.' I peeped out from under the blanket and what a horrible site, Boycey was sat on the toilet in the bathroom, bollock naked with the door wide open.

Eventually, I had to let him know who he was sharing a room with, then we carried on talking and it mainly consisted of reminding Boycey where we had been and what we had done the night before. He could not remember what he had done after leaving us but knew he had come back with Tommo.

I decided I needed to get up for breakfast. As I was searching for the trail of clothes and getting dressed, I discovered a major problem. I had left my trainers by the chair in the room and as I retrieved them, I discovered that one of them was soaking wet. It turned out that Boycey had not found the bathroom when he came in and had peed in the corner near the chair. Bizarrely it was only in one trainer – the right was bone dry, but the left was fully flooded. I also discovered that my jeans on the side of the chair had one wet leg on them.

At breakfast we swapped tales of the bedroom. In our room Boycey pissing in my trainer, in their room Toby fondling Dougie in a double bed all night.

Dougie says, 'He was fondling me all night. Putting his arms around me. He stroked my beard and called me Shirley!'

'Bollocks!' says Toby.

'Yes, your hands all over my bollocks,' says Dougie.

It was a bank holiday in France so all the shops were shut. I had not brought a spare pair of shoes so, after drying the trainer as best I could, all I could do was squelch around in it. We tried to find a hotel for the

Boycey – that's not a trainer!

night after the match but without success so we decided we would stay up all night and get the first train back to Beauvais and get one there first thing.

We went out for the day and bumped into quite a few others from Harrogate who had made their own way to Troyes. I believe one of these in the group with Spaz and Col Renicor was Bob Tappin, now of the documentary **Take Us Home** fame.

As it got nearer to match time, I donned the skeleton outfit and wore this to the stadium, as you do. Leeds lost 3-2 having won the first leg 4-2 so it was a hell of a tie even if it ended up far closer than it should have ever done.

After the game we walked back to the town centre and went to a bar for a few beers. We then went to a restaurant about midnight to pass the time as we were off on the early-morning train out of town – the first one was at 5am. We all had a steak in the restaurant but Tommo asking the

Rouse in the ground in a Skeleton outfit.

French for a rare one was a mistake. The one on his plate looked dazed and we were not sure it was even dead; it may have just been a flesh wound. The rest of our well-done steaks were fine, so we persuaded him to send it back.

We stayed in the restaurant for as long as we could and then found a late-night bar near the station but eventually we were on the streets with about two hours to go until the train. I was complaining that I thought by the time I got to Beauvais I would have a bad case of nappy rash from the squelchy-with-piss trainer. Of all the times to have your trainer pissed on, it had to be a day where I had no choice but to wear them for a full 24 hours!

We imitated tramps and hung around in doorways, even using our bags as pillows before boarding the train and getting to Beauvais. We could not believe what happened when we went to find a hotel, and we were told it was another town where they too only did double beds. What was it with the French and no single beds? I know they had a reputation for love and romance but they were really taking the piss out of us now.

We swapped partners so I had Everton Tommo while Boycey would try and intervene in Dougie and Toby's second grope-fest. After booking in we decided to have a kip as we had been up all night, then after that we went out in the afternoon. We managed to get a few hours of sleep then had a late afternoon and evening around Beauvais. It was a relatively quiet town but as usual we had a good laugh. We were not out too late as we were flying back to Prestwich quite early the next morning.

So another European trip was over, I had acquired a suit that helped me lose weight, suffered a bad case of nappy rash on my foot and Leeds could crack on in the UEFA Cup.

16

Zurich, 2001

The travelling party for Zurich was Rouse, Dougie Kaye, Roy Flynn, and Boycey. We flew to Geneva, and then took a train from Geneva to Zurich.

Everyone commented that in Geneva you could walk from the airport straight to a train. They also apologised via an announcement for the train departing 30 seconds later than the stated departure time. The journey was around three hours. We were enjoying a beer on the train and it was very scenic with views including lots of mountains and snow.

Dougie says to Roy, 'Just look at the scenery, Roy, it's a winter wonderland, what is it Roy?'

'It's a winter wonderland, Dougie,' replies Roy, as if they had rehearsed it.

It was very, very funny but, you must have seen the **Fast Show** sketch with Roy and his wife Renée to appreciate the humour.

We got to Zurich and wandered from the station to find our hotel. To our delight it was in a lively part of town with lots of bars and nightspots. Indeed, it seemed there was a club in the basement of our hotel building.

After checking in to the hotel we decided to check out the local area and have a few beers (I bet you are waiting for the story where I say we go to the local museum). We found a sports bar and met a group of eight Swiss football fans. One of them proceeded to tell us that they attended the FA Cup Final in England annually. One of them had been to the last 30 finals. They were very knowledgeable of British football.

I am not sure why, but we suddenly thought there had been no women in the bar, and there are eight of these Swiss blokes and they seem to be

Roy and Dougie.

coupled up; an older guy with a moustache and a younger lad. Another group of four Leeds fans entered the pub and started playing pool. When we pointed out that we thought it could be a gay bar they said, 'Well there is eight of us now, they might be thinking the same about us!' It was a good point well made. Anyway, as pleasant as the conversation had been, in the bar we decided to move on sharpish. It was not a scene Toby would have wanted to be a part of, so it was a good job he was not on the trip.

We had a few beers in the local district and it quickly became apparent that the whole area seemed like it was predominantly occupied by Latin South American people, mainly Peruvians, Brazilians and Colombians. There were some very good bars, but we ended up in a cosy little place that was like being in someone's front room. There was a female singer playing keyboards on in the bar, and Dougie thought she was fantastic. When she finished her show, he decided to talk to her.

'You were fantastic love. Come with me to England and I will make you the next Kylie Minogue!'

He was not expecting the reply, 'Fuck off! I hate Kylie Minogue.'

She was a lovely lass and had a way with words. We liked her straight talking but Dougie was now less keen on her.

We moved on to a few more bars and then decided to check out the club in the basement of our hotel building. It turned out it was a lap-dancing club. We got a beer, sat down at a table, and a couple of girls in bikinis were coming over to talk to us.

'We have spent all our money for the day so there is no point pestering us for a dance or money,' says Boycey.

'Bloody hell Boycey, you could have let them find that out for themselves, no need to tell them that!'

We had a final beer and headed up to bed. The new bedtime ritual following Troyes was implemented, 'Right guys, shoes on top of the wardrobe.'

The next morning, matchday, we had breakfast then were having a stroll in the local area when we came upon a shop.

'Is that you Boycey?' says Dougie.

There was a mannequin in combat trousers and a green jacket in the window, identical to the combat trousers and green jacket Boycey was wearing. The only difference was the gimp mask that the mannequin was wearing. Bizarrely, it was an outdoor clothing shop and not a porn shop or anything like that. We went in for a look around and there were mannequins looking like Boycey's brother everywhere. Boycey still has

Boycey brother, Boycey and Rouse.

the gimp mask after we chipped in. He says he keeps it in the special draw where Carol also keeps her leather gloves.

We had a few beers in the local bars and then as kick-off was getting nearer we jumped on a tram to the ground. We found a very small, glass-fronted bar near the ground with only room for about 20 people to fit inside. As they did not have any bouncers, Dougie decided he would appoint himself to the role as he did not want it getting too busy. He was refusing any locals entry and only letting Leeds fans in. Then a couple of Leeds stewards tried to get in.

'Have you got a match ticket?' he asked them.

'No of course we don't!'

'Well sorry, you cannot come in then!'

Dougie laughed when they wandered off and made a reference to the fact that one of them had stopped him getting in somewhere in 1956 or something.

After the fun in the new Leeds bar, we went to the ground. We were on the front row of the upper tier. Dougie must have been pissed up as at one point he was stood on the wooden fence at the front of the stand singing

Boycey and Dougie sending folk away from our bar.

whilst Boycey was holding on to him to make sure he did not fall. The same Boycey who had nearly died after falling down the stairs at home, and had been run over by a tram in Prague. We had all had a few so it did not seem worth pointing out the risks and he has since allowed Boycey to guard his ladder when he has been painting so it must have been okay.

Leeds won 2-1 so we returned to town well happy.

There was some trouble queuing for the trams, which seemed to be instigated by some young locals, so the Swiss are not as neutral as they make out. Getting off the tram at the other end we visited our little piece of South America and went to a few music bars. The others decided they were going back but I stopped out with some Leeds fans to go to another couple of bars. As I returned to the hotel a woman was in reception looking like she was about to leave. She came up to speak to me and she was a prostitute looking for business. I thought, Jesus, she was very old. I said, 'No, I do not want business but there is a bloke in the room upstairs that does. I can show you.' She followed me.

Getting upstairs, I said, 'He is in here,' and called Andrew (Boycey's name) and then sent her in. I was pissing myself laughing outside as I heard his reaction, 'Who the fuck are you? How did you get in here? I do not want business, no, now fuck off!! Get out of here you old witch, go on fuck off!!'

She swore at me, well from the tone of voice and string of words I guessed she had, as she left the room and I laughed and went in.

'Oh it's you, we should have known you were involved,' says Roy.

After we had breakfast the next morning, we went for a walk to see the lake before heading to the shopping area in the centre. It was a very posh and well to do. As Dougie always said, 'You could smell the mark-up.' Being a Sam Smith and happy hour sort of guy before the wallet comes out, we were stunned when Dougie took us in a pub in the centre and he bought the first round at £16 for four pints of Guinness. We decided Zurich must be Dougie's kind of town. We ended up staying in there all day and had eight pints. We were having banter with a group of Leeds

Dougie's round – Boycey, Rouse and Roy.

Boycey, Dougie and Rouse at Zurich lake.

Roy, Rouse, Boycey, Italian guy, Dougie and the Italian's wife.

fans who had come in. At one point a girl was asking for a job. One of the lads, who was sat near the door, pretended that he was the manager of the bar. He said, 'We have not got any jobs here, but our sister property has a few,' and he sent her off with directions to their hotel, saying there was a bar job there and to say he had sent her.

We went back to the local area via another few pubs and again visited the local music bars and clubs. We were not too late back as we needed to be up for the train to Geneva and the flight home early the next morning.

It was another of our great European trips, and I can highly recommend Zurich where we had found a small part of South America in Europe. Zurich was a very nice place even if it was on the expensive side, but even Dougie will pay for quality now and then – even if his career as an agent for foreign music talent hit the buffers. She could have been doing Kylie tribute nights all over Harrogate. The world would have been her lobster.

17

Dnipropetrovsk, 2002

The travelling party was Boycey, Toby, myself and Dave Tate. This was a strange game all around as we were traveling so far to the Ukraine and then playing Metalurg Zaporozhye, but in the city of Dnipropetrovsk at a neutral stadium.

We flew in to Kiev and from the airport got dropped by a taxi at the railway station. We were planning on getting an overnight sleeper train from Kiev to Dnipropetrovsk. I think Toby tried to ask a couple of taxi drivers if they would take us there and they looked at him like he was stupid. We had a few hours to spare before the train would be departing so we decided to sample the bars in the area near the station. Little Mick Hewitt from the Vine branch was at the station when we got there having just arrived too, so he came along with us. At the first bar we found we could not believe the price for the drinks. For five pints of the local beer, it cost us 45p. We had a couple of pints but then they somehow managed to explain to us that they had a wedding booked in and they needed to set up for it so we would need to leave.

We moved on around the corner and we came across a wooden building that looked like the sort of café you would see in the middle of a public park. It was on a patch of grass near some tower blocks and on a walkway that ran through towards the station. It was serving alcohol so we decided we would give the local vodka a go and bought a large bottle for the table to share, for about 30p. The orange to use as a mixer was more expensive than the bottle of vodka.

Boycey needed the toilet so he set off to find them. He did a lap of the central bit of the café where they were serving drinks and food. The

Blackpool with the Stan Bowles Calendar.

girl behind the counter was pointing over her shoulder. He went around again and tried a door that would take him into the kitchen. The girl took him to the exit door and pointed outside towards the bushes. There were no internal toilets, so it was basically find a tree or a bush outside. Little Mick was next to sample the outside toilets and he said, 'Its mixed. I was stood out there and three women just came behind the bushes and squatted down for a pee!'

We shared a few bottles of vodka and then decided it was time to start heading back to the station. On the way, as we walked past the first bar we had been, in we noticed that they were open again and serving so we decided to grab a last pint in there. We got a round of drinks. The wedding party was under way, and I remember one of our party having a dance with the bride. I think there must have been some wandering hands or something. I do not think we were quite run out of the place, but we were politely encouraged on our way.

We got to the station and the railway arrivals and departures boards were written in Russian, so we had not got a chance of recognising anything. We were almost giving up on finding someone who could speak English, it seemed no one did, when a young girl heard us talking. She offered to come with us to the ticket office and she helped us to buy our tickets for the train and showed us which platform to go to. We thanked her for her help, but she declined our kind offer of a trip across the Ukraine with us.

As we entered the platform, we met some other Leeds fans, Blackpool and his mate who thought we were all very drunk. They were not wrong.

We boarded the sleeper train; I was sharing with little Mick Hewitt in one room, Dave Tate on his own in the next one and Toby and Boycey in the room next to him. We bought some bottles of beer off the trolley that came along the train. In our room, Mick and myself were on the top bunks and two ladies had the bunks below. It seemed they did not speak a word of English. After a while one of the ladies waved and ushered us out of the room. She was miming the actions of taking her clothes off.

'Oh, she wants to get changed, that's why she wants us out of the room. She must be shy!'

As she was getting ready, we kept jokingly pretending to enter the room, 'Are you ready now?' We soon found out that she was not shy as when she had changed her clothes, she threw open the door as if making an announcement and was stood in front of us in a skin-tight lycra outfit that left nothing to the imagination. Everyone had been wrapped up everywhere you went so it was a shock to the system to see a very attractive young lady in lycra. We were allowed back in to the room. She and her friend opened a bottle of vodka and they decided they would share some with us.

A few minutes later the ticket inspector came in to our carriage and Mick, who had the tickets all together for the whole group, showed him them.

We were clearly distracted by vodka and ladies as we did not think about the others. The next thing we knew there was a huge commotion further down the carriage. There was screaming and shouting going on.

'That sounds like Toby and Boycey. Oh shit!' I said to Mick. 'You have their tickets. He will think they have not paid.'

I took the tickets and dashed to their room to find that Boycey had the ticket inspector in a headlock. Do not hit him, I thought, as I could see another spell in a foreign jail looming. I waved the tickets in the face of the conductor and convinced Boycey to let him go. The conductor had wanted to see their tickets and they were that drunk they could not remember where they were. The conductor had grabbed Boycey's leg to pull him off the top bunk. Boycey was recovering from a broken leg (he had run himself over with his own sit-on mower while cutting a grass bank), so was not best pleased and jumped down and had put the conductor into a headlock. Dave Tate had been in the toilet so when we explained that he was the fifth member of the group, the conductor was happy and went on his way. What happened next was quite incredible. About 15 minutes later the conductor returned with two bottles of beer to give to Boycey and Toby to apologise for the misunderstanding.

Ukraine railways clearly have a zero-tolerance policy when it comes to mistakenly harassing paying customers!

We arrived in Dnipropetrovsk very early the next morning. It was misty, and there were extensive roadworks under way on the streets. It looked like a war zone or a scene from an alien invasion movie. It felt quite strange wondering what sort of place we had come to. However, as we walked down the street the first thing that we saw in deepest darkest Ukraine was a yellow McDonald's sign. We were all starving so we went in for a breakfast. Blackpool and his mate came along. Some of our party could not remember meeting them in Kiev station the night before.

We got a taxi to the hotel to check in. Little Mick did not have a hotel, so he crashed with us and slept in a chair in the room (this was becoming a bit of a

18 Princes Gardens – Simon, Ian, Rob, Dave, Adrian, Mick and Eric.

habit as he had done this when I had met him in Glasgow in the early 1980s too). We got out and headed to the centre of the town where they had set up some beer tents for the Leeds fans. It was very quiet, so we had a couple of beers then moved on. We met a few local lads who had a drink with us and said they would show us where the ground was.

Eventually we made our way out to the ground with them arranging the transport for us. At the ground we found an off licence on a corner that was selling drinks. There were seven of us at this point and two large groups of Ukrainian football supporters, the Metalurg and Dnipropetrovsk fans. They were more bothered about each other than us and decided they were going to take a walk into the housing estate behind us to sort out their differences. Toby and Boycey could not keep their noses out of it and went with them for a look. It was all very strange as they formed a big circle and the two biggest guys on each side stripped to the waist. They then had a Greco-Roman wrestling match. Toby came back to where we were drinking and said, 'That's bloody rubbish, that is not fighting it's cuddling that, no punches or kicks, what's all that about. Rubbish!'

After a couple of beers, we went to the game. We were 1-0 up from the first leg and got a 1-1 draw to go through. The major incident in the ground was a story that a young Leeds fan was reported as having been sexually assaulted in the toilets, by one of the many varieties of uniformed soldiers on duty at the ground. It was chaotic to say the least. There was very little chance of working out who was meant to be running the stadium security. You could openly walk around the entire ground below the stand when you were off the actual terrace.

After the game, outside the ground one of the locals we had met turned up again like Mr Benn and said he was arranging the transport. A minibus then duly arrived, and they took us to a few bars on the edge of the town centre. There were the five of us and about 30 of them had managed to make it to join us. Each round for the whole group was somewhere between £5 and £6. Four of us had bought a round and then one of the Ukrainians came up to me and said, '//Your friend will not buy the drinks.'

I went up to Mr Tate and said, 'Dave, get the round in.' 'Fuck off, I am not buying for all these.'

'It's only about £5 for the round and they are being friendly! I am not sure annoying them is going to be a great idea.' Hearing it was only going to set him back a fiver he decided to get the beers in.

We went to a fair few more bars before deciding to bail out and head back to the hotel.

The next morning, after the late night with the Ukrainians we all had hangovers from hell. We had a lie-in and a late breakfast and then we set off for a walk. Just as we were all feeling like the need for a hair of the dog and wandering along a street I said, 'That looks like a bar up these stairs' 'Looks shut,' said Toby 'No, the door's open,' I said.

We walked up the stairs and through the door. It was like a club with a stage down the middle of the room but also a bar at each end. There was a bloke behind the bar, and we asked if we could have a beer. 'Yes, sit down,' he said. The only seats were along the edge of the wavy stage.

What happened next was one of the funniest things I have ever seen at 11.30am in an empty pub. The stage lighting came on, the music started blaring out and before we knew it there were about a dozen attractive ladies in the brightest, multi-coloured, fluorescent striped leggings and skimpy bikinis you have ever seen performing a dance routine for the five of us.

The dance routine was excellent, but I am not sure with hangovers from hell at that time in a morning it had been top of our bucket list of things to do.

A woman in a business suit had also come in to the bar and sat opposite. The girls came off the stage and were milling around us and the woman opposite. We left after a couple of beers. Toby said as we left, 'I am not sure how much tip I put in her knickers. I have not got a clue what these notes are could have been £50, £5 or 50p. It was too dark to see the money with my eyes.›

We were ready for lunch after our surreal experience, which even now still does not feel like it really happened. It was one of the funniest moments of my life and was quickly to be followed by another. We found a restaurant down the road and sat down to order food, but the menu was not readable as it was all in Russian. Cue Toby doing a series of animal impressions to try and order. He did the whole repertoire of beef, sheep, cow and chicken, and I am sure he even did the Basil Fawlty duck. The only one he did not do was his Moscow rabbit impression. The waitress was completely bemused. This went on for about ten minutes before I saw a table all having what looked like cooked breakfasts and just pointed and put four fingers up. The waitress was happy with that order, but I think she had lost the will to live.

Toby just said, 'I just wanted the pork sausage, egg and chips!'

'Well crack on with the impressions she might get it next week!'

We had our breakfasts and then we had to head in to town as we were getting the train back to Kiev. As we were walking back down the road the woman with the business suit was on the street and Toby decided he was going to try and chat her up. I did not have the heart to break it to him that he may not be her type. He was happy trying to get her to come back to Kiev with him.

After his failed bid at a romantic liaison, we carried on and got the train.

In another bizarre twist, one of the locals from the night before turned up on the platform and waited with us and then waved us off as the train departed the station. It really had been a strange but very funny place.

When we arrived back in Kiev the next day, we got booked into our hotel and headed off for our next day and night out. We had a good pub crawl around Kiev and then ended up in a bit of a bar with a club.

Boycey was being Boycey. The barman seemed to want us to have a vodka chaser with our pints, so we got a small glass of vodka to go with them. When it was Boycey's round he came back with a glass that was more like a half-pint glass.

'How did you get that?' I asked.

'I just kept shaking my head and saying bigger,' says Boycey, making finger movements to indicate a larger measure.

He proceeded to neck his and then grabbed mine when I was not looking and necked that too. To be fair it was quite good as it seemed to knock him out and we did not get a peep out of him for about an hour, which was unusual.

A couple of ladies came up and were talking to me and Toby. Toby had been doing his John Travolta **Pulp Fiction** dance to the music at the edge of the dancefloor. As I was stood next to the bar, I felt a prod in my ribs (Europeans seem to like that move) and there was a bloke with a beard in a polo neck black jumper.

'You are talking to my girlfriend,' he said. 'If you do not stop, I will stab you!'

Toby had wandered up to stand next to us with his arms folded. The bloke looked at him, looked at me and said, 'Who is this the bodyguard?'

I said, 'Does he look like Kevin Costner?'. It was lost on him, and I replied, 'No he is not but he can be if you want.'

I said, 'I will ask her and if she is your girlfriend then fair enough, but she came up to us If she isn't you can do one and do what you want.'

I think it is the first time I have been threatened by someone in a polo neck black jumper. I was expecting some Milk Tray.

She said she was not his girlfriend, which I relayed to him and told him to do one. We had a few drinks with them but I suspected they were just after westerners to pick up the drinks tab and Boycey was coming round, so we left and headed back to an area near the hotel.

As we got out of the taxi at the hotel, we could not seem to get the driver to understand us. He kept throwing the note back on to the passenger seat towards us when we tried to pay. Boycey got very frustrated and then next time it was thrown back he tried to throw a punch at the driver. I stopped him and pushed him away from the car. He landed on his backside on the floor outside the hotel entrance, so I told him he was drunk and that he needed to go in and that he needed to go to bed. For once he took the advice and cleared off to bed. It turned out we were giving the driver far too much money in his view and he did not want to take it off us. We found another note and he was happy.

Me and Toby were looking for a bar and were stood looking down the street to see if we could see any signs of one open when a bloke started talking to me. I thought he was talking in a foreign language until I got tuned into what he was saying.

'Hang on, you're talking English!' I said.

He had a broad Welsh accent. He was stopping in the hotel we were at and knew where the rooftop bar was so suggested if we wanted a drink that we go there. He took us up there for some more beers.

He was delighted when he heard we were Leeds fans. 'I am a Leeds fan from Swansea,' he said.

'Did you go to the Cardiff game?' he asked. 'I was ashamed to be Welsh.'

He was a little surprised that me and Toby declared it as one of best away games we had been to in a long time, a proper throwback game to the 'bad old days'.

We asked if he had come out for the game, but he had not. He was a divorced pharmacist and told us how he had split with his wife. They had now sold the massive, five-bedroomed house in which they had lived. He was on a trip where he had paid £180 and for that he got introduced to ten Ukrainian women who he could go on a date with. So he had paid £200 for his flight and accommodation and then £180 for ten names and addresses.

'So how does that work?' says Toby.

'I get the names and addresses and just arrange to take them on a date for a meal and a drink.'

Toby.

'Is that it?' says Toby. 'Don't you get to shag them?'

'No, just a date with them.'

'Well, I'd defo want a shag for £180!' declares Toby.

With us not having impressed him enough already with our class and sophistication, our Welsh friend was just telling us how he had met a lawyer, how she had the beauty and the brains, how she could be the one, and how he would invite 'you two boys' to the wedding. It was quite moving and romantic and then Toby started to struggle downing his vodka. He hiccuped a few times, then dashed off to the bog and returned with his shirt with a wide stripe straight down the middle like an Ajax shirt.

'I've been sick through my nose,' he declared. 'It was all vodka though.'

We decided we had maybe had a bit too much and had better get to bed as we were flying home the next day.

It was yet another brilliant eastern European trip and some brilliant memories that will live forever. We never did make the wedding, if it happened, so we will never know if the £180 was well spent.

18

Florence, 2002

The travelling party for the game against Hapoel Tel Aviv, which was played in Florence, was me, Charley Megginson, Dave Smith and his mate Adrian Craven from Hull, although a few others had made their own way over for the game too.

We flew from East Midlands Airport and unfortunately experienced a reasonably long delay which meant getting tanked up before we even got on the plane. We were flying to Venice. Chairman Charley in the city of love; what could possibly go wrong?

When we landed, we headed for our hotel as we were only staying in Venice for one night. I had been on a day trip to Venice previously when holidaying in Yugoslavia so seen the tourist bits, but never the main town itself which was just like any other city centre and no canals or boats around.

We checked in to the hotel and headed out to explore. We had a few beers and then went for a Chinese meal where we were first introduced to the Italian spirit, grappa. We were all given a shot of grappa by the waiter after someone was daft enough to ask what the strongest drink they served was. It can best be described as like drinking paint remover.

After we had finished the meal, we went back out for a few more beers. Smithy and his mate went back to the hotel earlier than me and Charley. We were sat in a bar when a group of about seven or eight Leeds fans from Beeston came in. I assume they were messing but one of them, the biggest lad, sat down at our table and was obviously trying to intimidate us. He was implying that they could mug folk and take what they wanted from them. I had my bottle under the table ready to wrap it around his head if I needed to, not that we had anything worth taking.

He decided he was joking and got up and left the table. Charley then had a bright idea and told them that we had discovered this wonderful Italian drink called grappa, and if you bought one you had to down it in one. One of their lads then decided he would get a round in, including one for me and Charley. 'Oh shit!' I thought to myself. 'They will now definitely want to kill us after this.' The lad did not order shot sizes – it was the Boycey Ukraine quarter-pint measures. 'Cheers,' the lad says. 'We all must down the grappa in one.'

Well, one of them, after downing his glass, has both hands over his mouth and is spewing through his fingers. Charley is inspired, they absolutely love this, and another two rounds of grappa follow to see who can hack it.

Charley blames the grappa on what he then describes as them going crazy. I am not so sure. The big lad calls over the Italian waiter.

'Yes sir,'says the waiter.

Pointing at the pool table in the back room the lad says, 'I want you to go out there get us one of those prostitutes off the street and we are all going to shag her up the bum on your pool table.'

'This is not possible,' says the waiter.

'How much of this silly money do you want then for it to be possible?' says the lad.

'No, absolutely no, this is not possible!' insists the waiter.

We finish our last round of grappa bought by me then me and Charley exit to go back to the hotel.

I am checking if the room key is at reception when Charley disappears. I get up to the room but there is no sign of him. Smithy and his mate say no, he has not been up to the room. I decide to get into bed when next minute there is a Chinese lad from reception knocking on the door.

'Please can you come and get your friend.'

I followed him and he took me down a couple of floors. There was Charley staggering around but doing a John Cleese impression of randomly tapping on the walls and the doors like he was testing them.

'What the hell are you doing, Charley?' I asked.

His eyes had gone though, something I have seen many times over the years. Once, when he fell and banged his head, I swear his eyes were rolling in different directions before they settled on the centre line like a fruit machine and he started hallucinating that he was in Bearwood Birmingham and people in (empty) parked cars were watching him. That night I put him in a taxi and said to the driver to take him home; tonight I had no choice but to take him up to the room.

We got in the room and he kept saying he wanted to go back out. He was babbling drunk. Smithy and Adrian told him to stay in bed. I was about nodding off when I heard a commotion, Charley was crawling on his hands and knees trying to make it to the door to escape whilst Smithy's mate Adrian was trying to stop him. 'For fuck's sake, you will get us all kicked out!' he said. I was laughing to myself then passed out. Apparently, this game went on for about another hour, so Adrian was fuming the next morning. He described it as far worse than anything he had encountered being at home with his three-year-old child.

The next morning, after breakfast, we headed for the train station as it was matchday and we were off to Florence for the game.

We checked in to our hotel and then hit the bars again. Whilst having a walk I decided to buy a present for the father-in-law, who was always cooking, I bought a knee-length apron, with a beautiful lady on it in bra, pants, stockings and suspenders. I bought two – one for him and one for me.

I decided mine should be worn for the day out and to the game, as you do! We had a few beers and then in one of the bars we bumped into another group of Harrogate travellers. John Reaveley, Roy Flynn, Boycey and his girlfriend Carol were in there. Boycey was at his obnoxious worst.

He was basically having a pop at her about everything. I was not sure if Boycey was showing off to prove that he would not change his behaviour just because Carol was there with him. Carol said that she was fine, that she wore the trousers, and it would be him in bother when she got him out of the bar later.

We were leading 1-0 from the home leg against Hapoel Tel Aviv and this night turned out to be a romp, 4-1, with Alan Smith scoring all four goals. The Leeds fans were on a big open bank down the whole side of the ground. I had my apron on and got a few strange looks from folk in the crowd. I was only worried when I walked past the Beeston lads who were sat in a group on the terrace, remembering what they had wanted to get up to in the bar.

There was a Perspex plastic fence around the stands, acting as a perimeter to the pitch, and I stood down there in the second half. It was down the Leeds left. It was very funny seeing Ian Harte and Harry Kewell do double takes as they retrieved the ball from the side of the pitch. They had clearly seen the apron and thought there was a woman in stockings and suspenders stood in the crowd next to the Perspex. Nice legs, shame about the face.

After the match we went in to Florence for the night out and whilst there are bits of it that are hazy, I can remember that eventually I was last man (in an apron) standing and I headed to a nightclub a little way out of town. The others had gone back. Surprisingly, I was allowed in to the club in my apron. I remember dancing with an attractive Italian girl, but she had insisted that if I wanted to dance with her, I had to take the apron off as she did not want to dance with a woman. I think I might have let her keep the apron as I certainly did not seem to have it when I returned to the hotel.

I walked back to the hotel about 4am, and the streets were deserted. When I entered the room, I found Charley lying on a bed with a pillow over his head. There was a right racket in the room.

'I have been trying to sleep for hours but I cannot for those bloody roadworks,' said Charley.

I went to the toilet but when I came out, I said, 'Hang on, what roadworks.'

'The ones in the street outside the hotel,' replied Charley.

'It is the middle of the night, it is 4am gone, there is no one working. There has not been for hours!' I said.

'Could it be this?' and I flicked the switch on the air conditioning unit and the noise instantly stopped.

'How long have you been in bed?' I asked.

'Since about midnight!' said Charley. 'That noise has been driving me mad!'

The next morning, we left Florence and headed by train to Pisa. We of course visited the Leaning Tower. We had a night around Pisa which involved us watching a very good rock band in the final bar we settled on. We stayed in the bar until late, partying in the music bar as there was a disco after the band finished.

Following our night in Pisa we flew home from Genoa.

Another top European trip concluded with Chairman Charley at his daftest. I am not sure Adrian had witnessed anything like it in his life.

I had some work commitments around the time we played Malaga in the next round, so Dougie and Boycey made that trip without me. I was confident we would progress but that was it, and after defeat at home in the second leg we were in freefall, and there were to be no more European campaigns and trips with Leeds.

In aid of

**Alzheimer's
Research
UK**

Make breakthroughs possible

Author's Acknowldegements

Thank you for buying and reading this book. I hope you enjoyed it. Mrs Rowson said she should write the closing remarks, but I said I would get back to her on that one. However, I should thank my family Val, Samantha, Jasmine, Tasha and Jamie for putting up with my Leeds watching over the years.

I have not covered every trip in the book as we had return journeys to Rome twice to play Roma and Lazio, Eindhoven and Maritimo again, a postponed trip to a match in Moscow to splay Spartak Moscow, and we then played them in Sofia a week later. We played Partizan Belgrade in Heerenveen, and we also had Champions League games in Barcelona and Istanbul, against Besiktas. I went to some but for others work got in the way (I'm not sure about money, wife and the kids).

I did do the club trips to Moscow for the called-off game and Deportivo for the Champions League quarter-final out of necessity and at times being the only Rouse Tours traveller.

I hope we have managed to get across the enjoyment to be had travelling Europe with your closest friends and all the Leeds family creating our stories and memories. As Toby said, 'We're not Leeds, we ARE Leeds!'

If our progress continues under Marcelo Bielsa or, I cannot bear to think about it yet, his replacement, then we may well be going on a

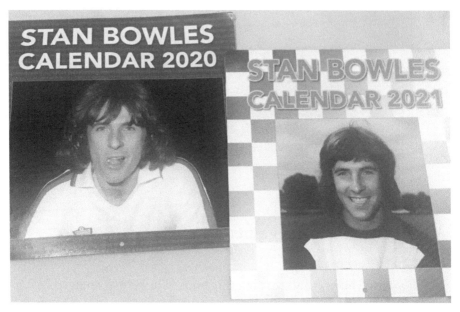

Stan Bowles, 2020 and 2021.

Nottingham and Harrogate Whites, Stan Bowles, 2020.

Tasha Rowson - lead in Legally Blonde, best singer in the family.

Come and get your picture with the Stan Bowles 2021 Calendar.

European tour again. I hope this has given you a feel for what may be ahead of us.

However, in this COVID world we are living in, being allowed to the pub and in the Elland Road souvenir shop would be a start, let alone the ground, away games and abroad. Hopefully better times are around the corner.

As I mentioned at the beginning of the book, we will be organising a fundraiser to support Alzheimer's Research when the COVID restrictions are lifted and hopefully with a return to Elland Road.

Watch out on social media for further information.

Twitter @daverowson

Facebook: Harrogate LUSC Whites

Website: Harrogatewhites.co.uk

If you wish to donate to Alzheimer's Research the website is https://donate.alzheimersresearchuk.org/publicnew

My thoughts and prayers are with all the Leeds United family
who have passed away or had loved ones pass away
during the pandemic.

Also remembering those friends of the branch we have lost recently

Harrogate Branch members
Eric Ware
Jeff Radcliffe
Mick Punt
Keith Major

Our Leeds players and legends
Jack Charlton
Norman Hunter
Trevor Cherry
Peter Lorimer
David Stewart

Marching on together, forever.

Best wishes,
Dave Rowson (Rouse)

ND - #0212 - 270225 - C0 - 234/156/9 - PB - 9781780916231 - Gloss Lamination